THE LIFE CYCLE LIBRARY

for Young People

The
Life Cycle
Library

for Young People

Book
2

Published by

PARENT AND CHILD INSTITUTE, CHICAGO

We are indebted to many professional organizations for their help and advice in preparing this set. Among the associations we wish to thank are: American Medical Association, American College of Obstetrics and Gynecology, American Academy of Pediatrics, and National Safety Council.

A NOTE TO READERS

The story told on the following pages is one of the most fascinating and important ones in the life of every human being. Doctors are still trying to unravel the enormous mystery of how a baby comes to be. They are still trying to discover the details of the process by which a tiny cell no larger than a speck of dust grows to be a growing, eating, crying, laughing, loving baby.

The pages that follow present the facts of this story as they are understood today. Distinguished doctors, psychiatrists, educators, and clergymen carefully checked the information presented here, and they have found it accurate. In the pages that follow, you will learn how you came to be, how you fit into the endless cycle of life, and what stages of that cycle lie ahead of you.

A special note to our girl readers

Many times in the pages that follow, the pronoun "he" actually means "he or she." It seemed sort of inhuman to call a baby "it," and it would have gotten rather tiresome to keep saying "he or she" when referring to a baby, so we adopted the standard grammatical practice of using the single pronoun "he." We want our girl readers to know that we value them, too; that we are not showing favoritism to boys.

THE EDITORS

In nearly every article you will find words printed in **bold face.** This special type is a signal that there is a glossary entry on this topic in the fourth volume. If you would like additional information about a word in bold face type, look for it in the alphabetical listing in the glossary.

At the end of many listings in the glossary, you will also find a note that tells you to look for a particular chapter or chapters in the first three volumes for expanded information. For example, after the entry on **birth** in the glossary, there is a note which will tell you that there is an entire chapter discussing birth in Book 2.

CONTENTS

8

THE BEGINNING OF A LIFE CYCLE

Life has changed dramatically for man over the past hundred thousand years. Yet the basic way the human life cycle begins and continues has not changed.

That basic way combines both 1) the natural, physical union of a man and woman, and 2) the social and emotional maturity of two human minds. Without physical union, the male sperm and female egg could not unite to begin the life of a baby. Without social and emotional maturity, parents could not give their children the many years of care necessary for children to grow up to be normal, well-adjusted adults.

For many thousands of years, people have recognized the need for long-lasting, secure families. **Marriage** is the way to guarantee that security. In a marriage, husbands and wives bring children into the world, and then care for them.

Through the ages, marriage has been an essential part of the human life cycle. Marriage satisfies a man's and woman's natural needs for affection and companionship. It also enables them to express sexual desires, which are a part of the human reproductive cycle, in a socially approved way.

In most modern countries, marriage is considered successful if it brings personal happiness to the husband and wife. In the United States, young people are free to select their own marriage partners, and love is a very important factor in that selection. Because of the need to obtain an education, most young people do not get married and have children until some years after the time nature has made them ready to reproduce.

Sexual maturity

By the time most people reach their late teens they are sexually mature and capable of beginning new life. The testicles of young men and the ovaries of young women are producing mature reproductive cells. All of the **reproductive organs** of both young men and women have enlarged to their adult size.

Sexual feelings, which are a normal part of physical maturity, become stronger in the teen years. These instinctive feelings are nature's way of making sure that men and women will someday unite to begin a new human life.

Most young people in their late teens and early twenties are capable of beginning life, but they realize that becoming

parents at this age could cause many problems. With increased maturity, they learn how to express their *sexuality* in a responsible way.

With dating experience and contact with many different kinds of people, young people gradually acquire better understanding of others. They grow in their ability to care for and love others. They mature physically, socially, and emotionally.

Meeting the right one

The years of adolescence help to prepare young people for marriage. Many young people, however, are mature enough to marry long before they do. Many of them want to finish college before they get married. Others want to be free to spend money on themselves, to enjoy travel, fashionable clothes, or a sports car before they get married. They are not in a hurry. Of all the different people they meet, one finally seems special and "marriageable."

Once such a young man and woman meet, it takes some time before they love one another. Each has probably had many friendships with people of the opposite sex, and has had affectionate feelings toward a few of those.

Very often the first attraction a couple feels is physical. Neither may be ideally beautiful or handsome, but each is physically appealing to the other.

After they have dated a few times, they find many other things which attract them to each other. They may enjoy talking about the same subjects; they may have similar work interests or have the same type of friends. Both may enjoy the same types of entertainments.

Most people generally associate with people who have similar levels of income, ways of living, educational backgrounds, and religious beliefs. Therefore, most couples who

become serious about each other share many similar ideas.

When mutual admiration and attraction continues, it frequently develops into the much deeper emotion of love. In most cases when a man and woman love one another, they wish to marry. As husband and wife, they are better able to do things together and to share the best experiences of life. One of the best experiences is having their own children.

Sexual intercourse

The most intimate way for a husband and wife to express their love is through sexual intercourse. Sexual intercourse is the act which enables the male sperm and female egg to unite to begin the life of a new human being. The primary purpose of sexual intercourse for all other living things is reproduction of the species. For a husband and wife, it is also an emotional and physical expression of love.

Before a husband and wife have sexual intercourse, they usually kiss and carress each other. Kissing and carressing expresses their affection and attraction for one another. It also causes them to feel a very strong sexual love and desire.

There are certain areas of the body, called *erogenous* or *erotic zones,* which are especially sensitive to kissing and carressing. Some erogenous zones, which differ slightly from per-

son to person, are the mouth, breasts, neck, tongue, and ears. The most sensitive areas are the genital areas. Both the tip of the husband's penis and the clitoris in the wife's vulva are very responsive to sexual stimulation.

Sexual stimulation helps prepare the bodies of both the husband and wife for sexual intercourse. When the husband is sexually excited, blood flows into his penis causing it to become stiff. This stiffening is called an *erection*. An erection enables a man to insert his penis into his wife's vagina.

When the wife is sexually stimulated, many tiny glands in the wall of her vagina give off a lubricating fluid. The wall also becomes relaxed, enabling the penis to enter.

Sexual intercourse begins when the husband puts his penis into his wife's vagina. The husband and wife lie close to each other in a comfortable position. During intercourse, the husband and wife move gently back and forth against each other. This movement causes the penis and vaginal wall to be stimulated.

When stimulation reaches a peak, the husband and often the wife too experience a pleasurable sensation called an **orgasm.** In the husband's orgasm, semen is spurted out of his penis into his wife's vagina. This release of semen from the penis is called an *ejaculation.* Just before ejaculation the prostate and seminal vesicles secrete fluids which mix with the sperm to form semen. About a teaspoonful of semen, containing millions of sperm, is ejaculated during orgasm. The wife's orgasm takes place when muscles of her vagina and uterus contract strongly.

If a sperm cell unites with an egg cell in the wife's body, the egg cell will be fertilized, beginning the life of a baby. The baby will begin to grow in the wife's body soon after fertilization, or conception. (The story of how a baby is conceived and grows in his mother's body is told in the next chapter.)

Fertilization does not occur every time a husband and wife have sexual intercourse. Frequently a married couple *make love*, as intercourse is often called, without planning to have a baby. They make love because it brings pleasure to both of them, and because it shows their love for each other.

Planning a family

Giving a great many children all the care they need is difficult. Therefore, many couples try to make sure they will not have more children than they can provide for. Today there are many methods of birth control, or **contraception**, which enable them to have sexual intercourse without conceiving a

child. These methods prevent the sperm and egg from joining together to create new life.

When a couple avoids having sexual intercourse during the days of the month when an egg may be present in a Fallopian tube, they use the *rhythm method* of birth control. The wife keeps a written record of her menstrual cycle, and tries to determine when ovulation should normally occur. Since many menstrual cycles are irregular and most women cannot be sure when ovulation takes place, the rhythm method is not entirely reliable. The rhythm method is the only method of birth control approved by the Roman Catholic Church.

There are many mechanical methods of preventing conception. One method is to use a physical barrier, such as a thin rubber cap or cup, which prevents sperm from getting to the egg. One of these caps is the *diaphragm.* The diaphragm is inserted by the wife into her vagina. It covers the entrance to the uterus, preventing sperm from entering the uterus. The *condom,* a thin rubber covering worn over the penis, prevents sperm from entering the vagina.

One other grouping of contraceptives is called *intrauterine devices,* or IUDs. IUDs are small plastic or metal objects which are inserted into the uterus by a physician or other trained medical person. IUDs come in many different sizes and shapes, such as rings, loops, or bows. Although they are effective in preventing pregnancy, doctors are not exactly certain how and why they work.

Oral contraception, commonly called *the pill,* is a very effective method of birth control. When a woman uses this method, she takes pills which contain female sex hormones. The almost daily intake of these artificial hormones causes the same kind of balance of hormones that would normally

RHYTHM METHOD FOR 28-DAY MENSTRUAL CYCLE

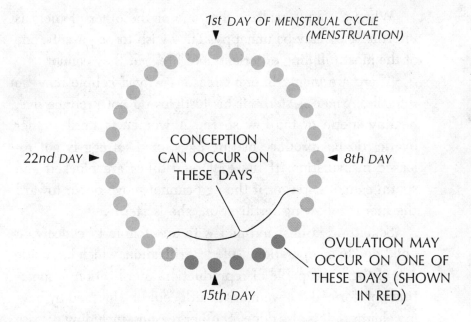

1st DAY OF MENSTRUAL CYCLE
(MENSTRUATION)

22nd DAY ►

CONCEPTION
CAN OCCUR ON
THESE DAYS

◄ 8th DAY

OVULATION MAY
OCCUR ON ONE OF
THESE DAYS (SHOWN
IN RED)

15th DAY

occur only during pregnancy. When a woman is pregnant, her hormones prevent the release of more eggs. The pill does the same thing, thereby preventing conception.

Many ideas for new methods of birth control are being investigated. Scientists try to find contraceptive methods which are totally effective in preventing pregnancy and which are also entirely safe.

Inability to have children

Almost all couples who marry wish to have children. They may want to control the number of children they have, but most do want to conceive and give birth to babies.

There are some couples however, who are unable to have children. This inability to reproduce, called both **sterility** and *infertility,* occurs in about one-tenth of all marriages.

When a couple realizes that one or the other of them is infertile, they may be unhappy. They wish to be parents, one of the most fulfilling experiences of life, but they cannot.

There are many different reasons why a couple may be infertile. A man is sterile if his testicles do not produce live, healthy sperm or too few sperm. A woman is sterile if her ovaries do not produce mature eggs, or if an egg is not released in ovulation. If the Fallopian tubes are blocked and sperm cannot enter, or if the egg cannot move down toward the uterus following fertilization, she is sterile.

Sometimes a husband and wife are unable to conceive a child due to an operation, called **sterilization,** which has made one of them incapable of reproduction. Sterilization is sometimes performed if a woman's health could be harmed by having children. It is also done for other reasons, including disease of the reproductive organs.

Sterilization in the wife occurs when her ovaries are removed (oophorectomy), or when her Fallopian tubes are cut and tied (tubal ligation). It also results when her uterus is removed (hysterectomy).

Sterilization in the husband occurs when his testicles are removed (castration) or when the tubes leading from his testicles to the urethra are cut and tied. This kind of sterilization (vasectomy) is not always permanent. In about 50 percent of all cases, the tubes can be rejoined in surgery and the man is made fertile again.

There are many other reasons why a married couple may be infertile. Fortunately, many couples can get medical help which will correct the cause of their infertility.

If they cannot become fertile and still want to have children, they can adopt children. There are many welfare agencies that handle adoptions. These agencies are run by people who are specially trained in adoption procedures.

People who are interested in adopting a child are carefully screened and interviewed by various people from the agency. Couples must meet certain qualifications concerning their age, background, and income. These procedures are necessary to be certain that a child will be placed in the proper home.

Adopting a child can be a wonderful experience. Childless couples who have adopted children say they love them as much as they would children to whom they had given life.

The life cycle

Nature guarantees that a man and a woman join together to create a new human life. Both sexes have strong sexual feelings which bring them together. Both also have male or female forms which make it possible for them to unite.

The strength of sexual desire and the pleasure of sexual union would not be enough to continue the human life cycle, however. For many people, life would be simpler without the responsibility of rearing children. But both men and women are influenced by their minds and emotions to *want* to become parents. When their children are older and mature, they also begin families—and new life cycles—of their own.

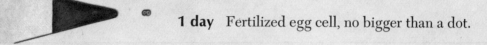 **1 day** Fertilized egg cell, no bigger than a dot.

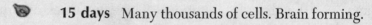 **15 days** Many thousands of cells. Brain forming.

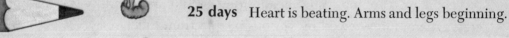 **25 days** Heart is beating. Arms and legs beginning.

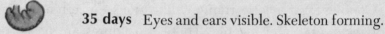 **35 days** Eyes and ears visible. Skeleton forming.

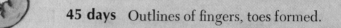 **45 days** Outlines of fingers, toes formed.

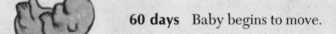 **60 days** Baby begins to move.

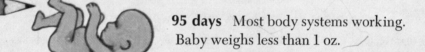 **95 days** Most body systems working.
Baby weighs less than 1 oz.

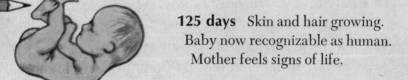 **125 days** Skin and hair growing.
Baby now recognizable as human.
Mother feels signs of life.

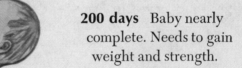 **200 days** Baby nearly
complete. Needs to gain
weight and strength.

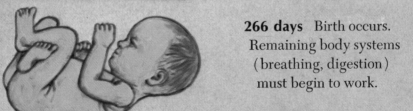 **266 days** Birth occurs.
Remaining body systems
(breathing, digestion)
must begin to work.

9

HOW
A BABY
DEVELOPS

Everyone has one special day in the year that he celebrates—his birthday. It represents the day he was born.

Actually, each person's life begins before the day he is born. It begins about nine months earlier in his mother's womb. A baby who has just been born is not really a brand new person.

A baby's life starts from one cell smaller than the dot at the end of this sentence. During about 266 days the cell divides into many billions of cells, forming all parts—the skull, the heart, and so on—of a baby's body. The original cell becomes a full-size baby weighing about seven pounds.

The period of growth before the baby's birth is called the *gestation period*. During the gestation period a baby grows from something as small as a speck of dust to a baby about 20 inches long.

A baby grows faster during the first nine months of his life than he ever will again. All of this rapid growth takes place *prenatally*—before a baby is born. The newborn really has a life story.

A new life begins

Human life begins when a sperm cell from a father enters and fertilizes an egg cell of a mother. This joining of two cells is called **fertilization** or *conception*.

Fertilization occurs only if a sperm cell meets with an egg cell in one of the **Fallopian tubes** soon after sexual intercourse. Only one egg is normally released each month, and an egg can survive only about 24 hours if it is not fertilized. Sperm can survive in the Fallopian tubes for at least two days after intercourse. For these reasons, there are many days during the month when fertilization cannot take place.

Once sperm cells are in the vagina, they have a long path to follow. They must pass through the cervix, travel up through the uterus, and then enter the "correct" Fallopian tube. ("Correct" because only one tube contains an egg each month.) The trip is only about 6 or 7 inches long. Yet, because sperm are so extremely tiny and meet with so many hazards along the way, the journey is difficult.

Of the millions of sperm deposited in the vagina during sexual intercourse, only one will be able to unite with an egg. Many sperm cannot survive the acid condition of the vagina.

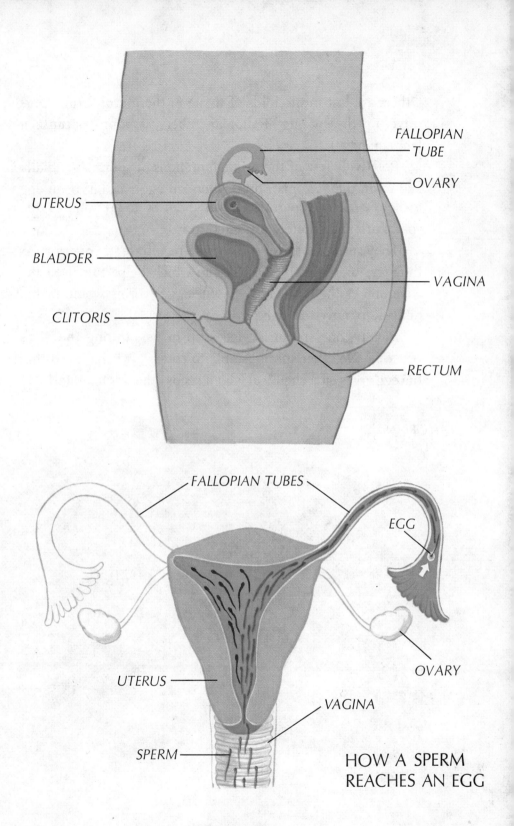

FALLOPIAN
TUBE

OVARY

UTERUS

BLADDER

VAGINA

CLITORIS

RECTUM

FALLOPIAN TUBES

EGG

UTERUS

OVARY

VAGINA

SPERM

HOW A SPERM
REACHES AN EGG

Others are lost in the folds of tissue in the uterus. Still others travel up the "wrong" Fallopian tube. ("Wrong" because it lacks an egg.)

Relatively few of the original millions of sperm eventually end up in the Fallopian tube where an egg will be. If an egg is there when the sperm arrive in about 30 to 90 minutes, the sperm are immediately attracted to it.

They surround the egg and try to penetrate its covering. As they try, they give off an enzyme which helps to soften the covering. Without this enzyme, the egg covering would be too difficult to move through.

Finally, one sperm is successful in penetrating the egg's covering. No other sperm is able to enter. (It is believed that the egg gives off a chemical which keeps others from entering.)

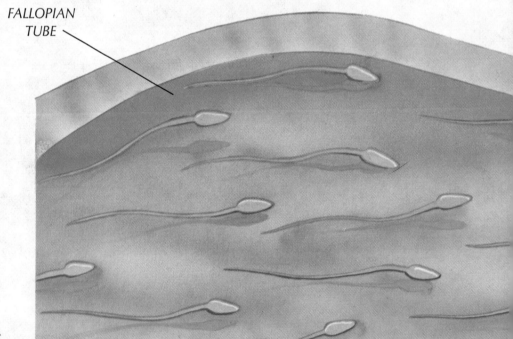

FALLOPIAN
TUBE

At the moment that the nucleus of the sperm unites with the nucleus of the egg, fertilization takes place.

Together, the sperm and egg create a new human cell. This tiny cell will begin to divide as it moves to the uterus.

Heredity of the new life

In both the **sperm** and the egg, or **ovum,** is a center called the nucleus. The nucleus has **chromosomes** which determine whether the new human will be tall or short, have small or large bones, have blue eyes or brown eyes, and many other things. At the moment of conception, the chromosomes of the sperm cell and the egg cell come together, and the traits which the child will inherit from his parents are determined.

SPERM

EGG

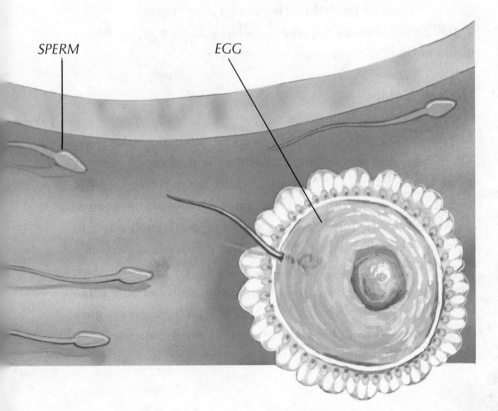

Both mother and father contribute equally to the child's heredity—with one exception. It is the father's sperm which determines whether the baby will be a boy or a girl.

Every sperm and egg cell has 23 chromosomes. One of these 23 is a sex chromosome. The sex chromosome in the egg cell is always female. The sex chromosome in the sperm cell can be either male or female.

When a sperm with a male chromosome (called a "Y" chromosome), fertilizes an egg, the baby will be a boy. When a sperm with a female chromosome (called an "X" chromosome), fertilizes an egg, a girl is created.

The sex of a baby, therefore, is determined at the time of conception. Which kind of sperm fertilizes the egg is a matter of chance, and nothing that happens after conception can change the sex of the baby. There is no easy way for a doctor to tell a mother-to-be whether she has a boy or girl growing inside her. She simply must wait and see.

The cell divides

After conception the fertilized egg splits into two similar cells. These two cells divide into four, then eight, then 16, and so on at a tremendously fast rate. While the fertilized egg is dividing, it moves along the Fallopian tube toward the uterus.

All cells of the fertilized egg are attached to each other in a cluster. Once in a while, the egg first divides into two cells that do not remain attached. They separate, and each then continues dividing on its own. These two cells become **identical twins**. Identical twins look almost exactly alike because they are formed from the same original ovum and sperm. They are always the same sex, either two boys or two girls.

146

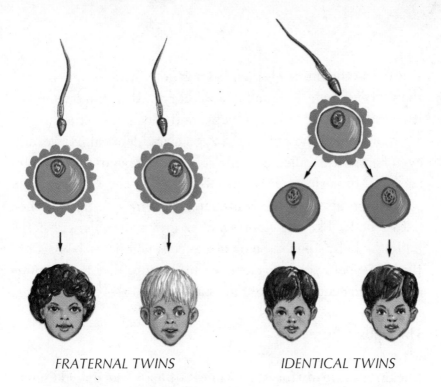

FRATERNAL TWINS   IDENTICAL TWINS

Fraternal twins are created when a woman's ovaries release two eggs at the same time. If each of these eggs is fertilized by sperm, two babies will start to grow. Fraternal twins are formed from two different fertilized eggs. Therefore, these twins look no more like each other than other brothers and sisters. They may be of the same sex, or different sexes.

The baby begins to grow

The cluster of cells reaches the **uterus** about a week after conception. Once there, it attaches itself to the lining of the uterus. Although by this time it is made up of a few hundred cells, it is still no larger than a grain of sand.

Throughout the first month of prenatal life, the baby-to-be does not look like a human being. While just a cluster of cells

147

floating to the uterus, it is called a **zygote.** After it attaches to the uterine lining, it is called an **embryo.** After three months, it looks like a tiny, scrawny baby, and is called a **fetus.**

At first all of the cells of the zygote are identical. However, even before it is called an embryo, the cells begin to "specialize," and to perform different jobs.

One group of the cells prepares to form one part of the baby's body, like the skin. Another group of cells will help build the baby's bones. Some of the cells will never be part of the baby. Their job is to create certain "tools," like the **amnion** and the **placenta,** that help the baby develop.

The baby's home

The uterus is ready for its new guest. It has a bloodfilled lining waiting to receive the embryo. This is the lining that is built up every month during a woman's menstrual cycle.

When a woman is not pregnant, she has a monthly menstrual flow, and the uterus sheds its lining. However, as soon as there is a fertilized egg in a woman's body, things change. The ovary receives a signal from the egg to continue producing **progesterone.** Progesterone is the hormone that builds up the uterine lining. A pregnant woman does not have another menstrual period until after her baby is born.

At the beginning of pregnancy, the uterus is about the size of a small woman's fist. As the baby grows inside it, the uterus stretches. During the early months of pregnancy the embryo is so small that it can move freely in the uterus. In the last months, when the baby is large, the uterus is a snug fit, even though it has become much larger. The baby is held securely as though he were wrapped in a warm blanket.

Between the wall of the uterus and the baby is a membrane. The membrane, called the amniotic sac, is formed from some of the cells which grew out of the fertilized egg.

The amniotic sac is filled with liquid, and the baby floats gently and comfortably in this warm bath. This fluid prevents the baby from being jolted or bounced around by his mother's movements.

The baby's lifeline

All of the baby's needs are taken care of by the placenta and the **umbilical cord.** The placenta is a flat mass of tissues and blood vessels that is fastened to the wall of the uterus.

In the early months the placenta is larger than the tiny embryo. The placenta gets as big as it will ever be during the sixth month of prenatal growth. By that time it has grown from a small cluster of cells to a flat, round piece of tissue shaped like a large, fat pancake. It weighs about one pound.

Growing out from the placenta is the umbilical cord, which is attached at what will later be his belly button. While the baby grows in his mother's uterus, he and the placenta are always connected by this cord.

The umbilical cord is like a sturdy but bendable rubber tube. It is only a fraction of an inch long in the first month of prenatal life. By the ninth month, however, it has grown to about 20 inches.

The umbilical cord is long enough so that the embryo is not tied down to one place in the uterus. The cord can twist and untwist when the embryo moves around. The embryo is much like an astronaut who leaves his spacecraft to take a "space walk," but is always tied to his spacecraft by a cord.

The main purpose of the placenta and umbilical cord is to nourish the growing baby. They send it food and oxygen from the mother's blood. The mother's blood never goes directly to the baby. The baby has his own blood system that is separated from his mother's by a thin wall of cells.

The baby's blood goes from his body into the umbilical cord. At the far end of the cord the blood picks up oxygen and food from the placenta and then returns to the baby.

The placenta gets oxygen and food from the mother's blood. The food is not the kind of food a person eats. It is nutrients made by the mother's digestive system and sent into her blood.

The baby uses the oxygen and food, and waste products are created. These waste products pass back through the cord and placenta. There they are absorbed and discarded by the mother's body.

The placenta is also a protection for the child. It filters out from the mother's blood many harmful germs or drugs which might hurt her baby.

The first month—1 to 30 days

While the placenta is growing, the embryo is also growing very fast. The one-month-old embryo has the start of a head, a body, and a little tail. The tail gets smaller as the embryo's body grows, and finally the tail disappears. It becomes part of the end of the backbone.

The baby's head is almost as long as his body at the end of the first month. He has the beginning of a brain.

The baby's tongue has started to form. He has four dark buds at the places where his arms and legs will grow. Almost

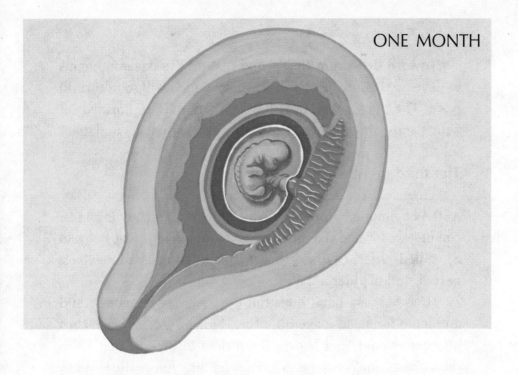

every body organ has started to develop and the embryo is 10,000 times larger than the fertilized egg. Yet it is only one fourth of an inch long!

By the end of the first month there is a heart (shaped like a tube) that is beating and circulating blood. Some of the blood is made in a small sac hanging from the embryo, called the "yolk sac." The yolk sac is now as big as the baby, but it will later get smaller and disappear.

The second month—30 to 60 days

The two-month-old embryo is still tiny, but it is beginning to look like a human baby. It is one inch long and weighs about 1/30 of an ounce, about as much as two aspirin tablets. Even though he is very small, the embryo has a human face with eyes, ears, nose, and lips. He also has the start of a neck.

151

Toward the end of the second month, the skeleton begins to develop. It is made of soft cartilage which will soon turn to bone. The baby's tiny arms have grown and are finished off with hands and fingers. The baby has legs, feet, and toes.

The third month—60 to 90 days

At the beginning of the third month, the baby's body is almost completely formed. He now looks enough like a real baby to be called a fetus. Brain, heart, lungs, stomach, intestines, nerves, and bladder are all there.

He is not very handsome, but eyes, ears, nose, mouth, and a bulging forehead make up a tiny, human face. He can turn his head, squint, and frown. From time to time he may even show what looks to be a smile on his funny little face.

His muscles work, and he can "swim" around in the sac which holds him. Up until the third month, his movements are jerky, like a mechanical toy doll. After that, his movements are more graceful. By the end of the third month, he can kick his legs, turn his feet, curl his toes, move his thumbs, and turn his head.

Although the fetus moves around a great deal, the mother rarely feels these movements until the fourth month of her pregnancy. The baby is still too small for his movements to be felt. He still weighs less than one ounce.

In the third month, the fetus cannot yet suck, but he can swallow. He gulps the amniotic fluid. Some of this fluid is expelled through the baby's kidneys. This urine is perfectly clean because it is never exposed to air or bacteria.

The baby does not drown in the amniotic fluid. He gets

the oxygen he needs through the umbilical cord from his

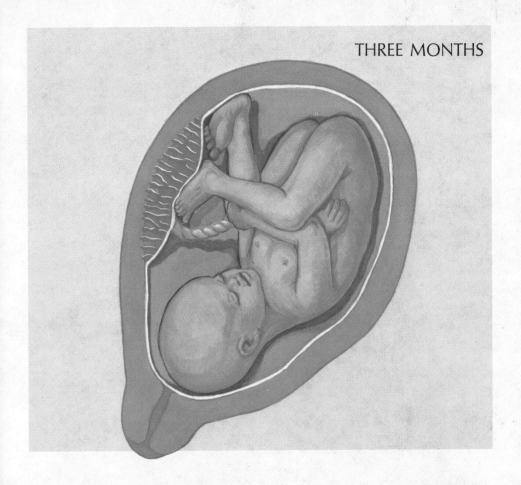

mother's blood. He practices breathing, but his lungs are filled with liquid. This liquid will be forced out of his lungs when he is born and starts breathing air.

During the first three months, the fetus grows into a well-formed, tiny baby. In the next months it grows longer, adds weight, and gains strength.

Fourth, fifth, and sixth months—90 to 180 days

The fourth month is a month of huge growth. The fetus adds about ten ounces to his weight and five inches to his height.

153

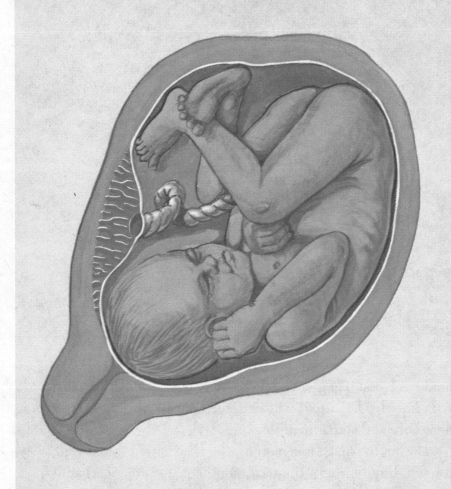

In the fourth month the mother may feel a slight flutter in her abdomen. This flutter is called the "quickening"—the first sign of the new life inside her.

By the fifth and sixth months the mother definitely feels her baby kicking and churning about. These movements do not hurt her, but they sometimes feel like good thumps.

The fetus floats in the sac and can perform like an acrobat. He turns from side to side, rolls over, somersaults, kicks, and swings his arms and legs.

Fortunately, the baby's umbilical cord does not get knotted during all this moving around. The cord is too stiff to knot because of the force of the blood rushing through it. The cord is always wet, and it slips over the baby's body as he moves.

By the fifth month the baby has a thin layer of skin which is wrinkled because of the water he floats in. When the baby later gains fat, his skin smooths out. At birth, he is covered with a cold-cream-like substance, called the **vernix**, that protects his skin. The vernix is washed off soon after birth.

Hair begins to grow on the body of a five-month-old fetus. It grows on his arms, legs, and back. This usually disappears during the sixth month, when hair starts to grow on his head.

Seventh, eighth, and ninth months—180 to 266 days

During the last three months of prenatal life, the fetus gains most of his weight. At the beginning of the seventh month he weighs about two pounds. By the end of the ninth month he weighs about seven pounds. He also grows from about 14 inches at seven months to around 20 inches at birth.

The fetus practices sucking during the last three months of prenatal life. From time to time he may suck his thumb.

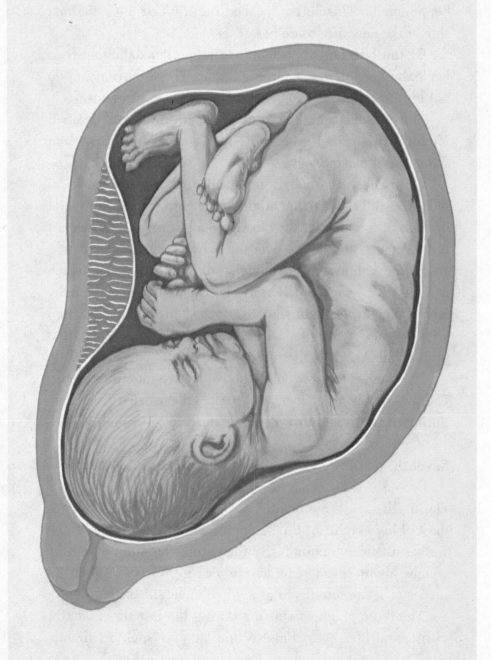

(A baby's thumb and other fingers already have nails. A baby's finger nails usually need cutting immediately after birth.) Often a mother will feel a knocking in her abdomen. This is the fetus hiccuping.

By the seventh month, the baby is developed enough to live if he should be born early. A premature baby must have special hospital care, and is kept warm and protected in a heated incubator.

During these last months the baby gains the fat and strength he needs to live on his own in the outside world. All his body functions are prepared—his blood is constantly being circulated, his muscles are developed, and his digestive system is ready for his first meal.

The ninth and final month is a time of waiting for both the mother and her baby. The mother is probably feeling clumsy and awkward with her large belly. Her baby moves very little because his full size takes up most of the room in the uterus. Most babies settle into a head-down position, ready for birth.

At the end of about nine months, the fetus is ready to live outside the uterus. The first stage of his life story is completed. He has grown from one to over 200 billion cells. His body has developed from a single cell to a masterpiece of efficiency.

As an embryo and a fetus, he has been growing and practicing all the things he must do after he is born. He is ready for the next stage of his life. He is a baby who can live and grow outside his mother's body.

10

THE
MOTHER
OF THE BABY

The young husband rushing with an extra pillow and helping his pregnant wife into a chair is a familiar scene in movies and TV family series. His special care of his wife is understandable, but usually it is not necessary. Special care is needed, yes, but not the kind given an invalid.

Pregnancy is not a disease; it is another stage of life. Like puberty and birth, it is part of the regular process of living. Puberty makes pregnancy possible, pregnancy is giving life, the new life grows on to puberty, adolescence, and adulthood.

Each of these stages is a change. Pregnancy is a change, because a life has been created and is growing within the uterus of the mother. Nothing is newer, more changed than the creation and development of a new life.

Pregnancy, however, does not need to call for a change in the way the mother eats, sleeps, works, or takes part in sports or other activities. None of these things needs to change if the mother is reasonably healthy and has good living habits. If she is in good physical condition and stays that way she can learn, with her doctor's help, how to accommodate her way of living to her changing body as her baby grows inside her.

Preparing for parenthood

The time for a couple to begin **prenatal care,** including medical care, is not after the wife thinks she may be pregnant. Preparing for parenthood should begin when marriage begins. It should continue as long as the couple is planning to have children. Preparing for parenthood simply means following good practices in diet, rest, exercise, posture, and cleanliness.

These rules may vary somewhat from person to person. If a couple has any question about proper health practices, they should see a doctor.

For some couples, the first child will come early in marriage. Other couples, especially if the wife has a career, may hold off having a child for several years. At whatever time a man and wife are planning to have a baby, they each should have a thorough physical examination. There are two reasons for seeing the physician early.

First, the doctor can determine if there are any physical conditions that could hamper conception. He can also find out if there are any conditions that require special medical care, or might make it wise for the couple not to have children.

Second, such a visit will alert the physician that the couple is trying to conceive. He can then avoid using X-rays, certain drugs, or other treatments that might interfere with conception or with a developing baby. He can also advise the couple to avoid medicines or activities that might interfere with conception and pregnancy.

Time to see the doctor

Missing her menstrual period is the first sign that a woman might be pregnant. But for a more sure sign of conception there must be other symptoms, too.

She may notice that her breasts are tender. They may have a tingling feeling, and they may seem to be a little larger. She may feel sleepy more of the time, or grow sleepy more easily in the evening. It may seem that suddenly she needs to urinate more often. Perhaps her husband will ask if she is getting enough rest. Someone may say that she looks a bit pale.   161

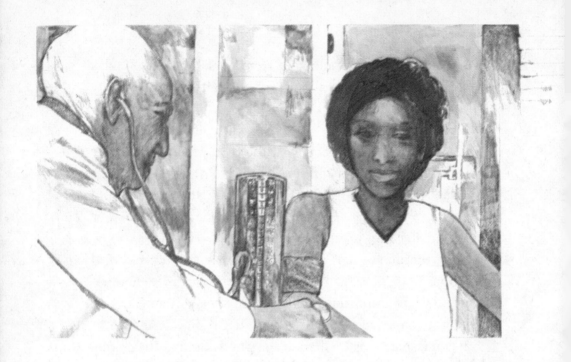

If any one of these symptoms occurs in addition to the missed period, the woman should see her doctor. He will conduct a test to determine if she is pregnant. This test is a simple one, and consists of an analysis of her urine.

On that first visit, the doctor will also probably give the woman several kinds of examinations. These will include a physical examination, blood and urine tests, and usually a pelvic and vaginal examination.

He will check her blood pressure, and will take a blood sample. The blood sample will be tested for anemia and syphilis, as well as for blood type and **RH factor.**

If the blood is anemic, it cannot carry enough oxygen for both the mother and baby. If there is syphilis or other venereal disease, the doctor will treat the disease.

Knowing whether the mother has blood type A, B, AB, or

O is important in case a transfusion is needed during the pregnancy or delivery. Knowing the mother's Rh factor can be a matter of life and death to the coming baby. In rare cases, the Rh factors of mother and baby are incompatible. The doctor can treat Rh incompatibility if he knows the condition exists. The important thing is to learn the mother's Rh factor at this first examination so that if treatment ever becomes necessary he will know what to do.

The Rh factor is a term used to describe a type of protein present in the red blood cells of most people. When this protein—called *D*—is in the cells, the blood is called *Rh positive*. When a slightly different protein—called *d*—is in the cells, the blood is called *Rh negative*. (The factor is named for Rhesus monkeys, who also have this protein.)

More than 85 per cent of women are Rh positive. The rest are Rh negative. If an Rh negative mother is married to an Rh positive father, there is a chance that a problem will arise for the baby. If the baby inherits the mother's Rh negative blood, no problem will develop. But if the baby inherits the father's Rh positive blood, there is a chance that a problem could arise.

The mother and the baby have separate blood systems, and the two do not normally mix. Yet, if some blood from an Rh positive baby passes through the placenta to an Rh negative mother, the mother's body may produce antibodies against the strange D protein. These antibodies may travel back through the placenta, causing harm to the baby.

163

If the mother is Rh negative and the father is Rh positive, the doctor will be alerted. He will keep a constant close watch for antibodies in the mother's blood. If they appear, he will take the necessary steps to protect the baby.

Checking the growing space

In addition to the general examination and the tests of blood pressure, urine, and blood, the doctor may make, on this first visit, a pelvic examination. If he believes that such an examination is not yet necessary or may cause a possible hazard for the embryo, he may postpone it for the next visit.

The purpose of this examination is simple but important. It is to see whether the developing baby will have room enough to grow and to be born. He will measure the **birth canal**, the passage from the **uterus** through the **cervix** and **vagina** that the baby will pass through in birth.

Many questions

Before the first examination is over, the doctor will give instructions to the woman about her diet, rest, exercise, use of medicines, symptoms to watch for, weight gain, and dental care, if needed. The woman may ask him about other matters that may concern her, including exercise, working, sexual relations, traveling, maternity clothing, and the use of tobacco and alcohol.

Then, there will still be one more important question: When is the baby due?

Calculating the due date is not as hard as finding a needle in a haystack. Since birth usually comes about 280 days after

the first day of the mother's last **menstruation,** the doctor asks the mother the first day of her last period before pregnancy, and figures from that date. But the physician should not be criticized if the baby is not born on this date. The odds for a baby arriving exactly on the day predicted are about one in 12. The chances of labor beginning even within a week of the estimated due date are only 50/50.

Nine months to a new life

It is important that the expectant mother keep all the appointments scheduled by her doctor during her pregnancy. At each examination the doctor or his nurse will weigh the mother, take her blood pressure, examine the abdomen, test the urine, and perhaps check the blood for anemia.

An expectant mother must get a completely well-balanced, non-fattening diet, starting in the first month of pregnancy, even if she never has before in her life. The most important nutrients for the baby are proteins, minerals, and vitamins. Scientists believe that lack of these nutrients can cause the baby to be smaller and weaker, and may even interfere with the growth of his brain. This is especially true when the poor nutrition comes in the last few weeks before birth, or in the first few months after the baby is born if breast fed.

Among the basic nutrients both the mother and the developing baby need are *protein* to build and repair both bodies; *vitamins* and *minerals* to keep the muscles, bones, and organs working well and growing; and *carbohydrates* (starches and sugars) and *fats* for energy.

To make sure that she gets enough of these important nutrients each day, a woman should get food from all four basic food groups. These groups are (1) meat or other protein, (2) fruits and vegetables, (3) milk and dairy products, and (4) breads and cereals. Because the mother needs more nutrition as the baby grows larger, she needs even more of these foods in the last four or five months of pregnancy.

The increasing size of the uterus during the later stage of pregnancy may cause some women to have digestive upset. The stomach and intestines may be squeezed into such a small area that a woman cannot comfortably eat even normal quantities at one sitting. This may be especially true for a woman carrying more than one baby. If a woman has trouble eating normal quantities, more frequent smaller meals may be the answer. Some doctors advocate not just three meals a day, but four, five, or six small meals or three moderate meals plus two or three small snacks.

During the first three months of pregnancy, some women do not gain much weight, and may even lose a little. If there is a tendency to gain, though, the increase should be limited to 1½ pounds a month. From the third to sixth months, gains will be more rapid, and should be held to 1½ to 2 pounds a month.

Some doctors say that the total gained by the end of the sixth month should be about half the total pregnancy weight gain. During the last two or three months, the rate of gain is about 3 pounds a month, caused mostly by gains in the baby, the expanding womb, and the amniotic fluid.

Aside from generally trying to control her weight, the only kind of gain that should worry an expectant mother is any sudden gain of several pounds in a short time. If this happens, the doctor should be told immediately.

Feeling well, being well

Pregnancy should be a time of feeling well. Pregnancy is not a time to change a woman's whole way of life, and this includes life's pleasures. She should continue to do the things she enjoys.

If a woman smokes, however, she should be aware of the results of smoking. Heavy smoking of cigarettes may cause premature birth, excessive weight gain, or increased blood pressure in the mother.

Alcohol is not forbidden to mothers, but they should not drink much. If a mother enjoys a drink before dinner or a glass of wine with the meal, she can continue having it—that is, *a* drink. Drinking more than one average cocktail or highball or more than one glass of wine or beer is not encouraged by doctors.

If a women has a job and feels well while doing it, there is usually no medical reason why she should stop working. If she can keep working through the first three months of pregnancy, she probably will be able to continue through the remaining months as well. Her employer, however, may want her to

stop working during the middle months of pregnancy. A normally healthy woman can do what seems reasonable to her, without fear of harming herself or her baby. This is true both at home and in the office. Her doctor determines if she should limit her activities. He will restrict her activity only if there is some danger to herself or to her baby.

If possible, though, she should try to lie down at least twice a day with her feet up. This same rule also applies to women keeping house in their homes.

Rest, exercise, and travel

If a woman normally gets about eight hours' sleep during a night, she should continue to do so. Less than eight hours' sleep a night usually is not enough for anyone, whether pregnant or not. More sleep at night may be very pleasant for the expectant mother, but it alone will not meet all her needs for rest.

An expectant mother should rest at least twice a day, in the morning and in the afternoon. Each rest period should be no less than 10 to 15 minutes. A total of an hour or an hour and a half is better, divided into morning and afternoon rest periods of 30 to 45 minutes each.

While resting, the mother should loosen or slip off her outer clothing, lie down, and put her feet up so that circulation through her body can be at about the same level.

If a woman enjoys a sport or other physical activity, she can continue to enjoy it while pregnant as long as the activity does not cause her to be uncomfortable. This applies to gardening, swimming, hiking, cycling, dancing, golf, or horseback riding.

She should not, however, take up a new sport which would be extremely strenuous. Skiing, for example, would put a strain on muscles which were formally unused or used differently. This sport, then, might be dangerous for her.

Throughout pregnancy walking is always good exercise. It should be brisk walking, though, not a casual stroll.

A pregnant woman should not exercise in any way that is uncomfortable, overexerting, or tiring. When she is within six to eight weeks of the due date, it is best to avoid any strenuous activities, regardless of what they are.

Early in pregnancy, if a woman does not get travel sick, any form of travel is all right. As pregnancy continues, some changes may be needed. Perhaps she will not be comfortable traveling more than 150 miles or so by car. On auto trips it is a good idea to stop about every 50 miles to let her stand, walk about, and stretch.

After the seventh month, because of the possibility of premature birth, it is best to travel by the fastest means possible so that if medical care is suddenly needed it can be reached in time. When she gets to the ninth month, it is best to travel only short distances by car, and to stay close to home and the doctor.

Clothing for the expectant mother

As the body gets larger, maternity brassieres and girdles should be worn to support the heavier tissues and organs and to make the mother feel less fatigued. The pregnant woman does not need to wear shapeless maternity dresses that look like flour sacks. Maternity clothing is available in the latest styles at department and maternity clothing stores.

If a pregnant woman likes to wear high heels, she can. Later, when she is bigger and heavier (when the baby has grown), she can best judge whether low heels are better for her.

Things to be avoided are tight-fitting, restricting clothing, including tight belts and round garters that restrict blood circulation. As long as an expectant mother maintains good grooming and good taste, she can wear any style of clothing.

Prenatal exercise classes

Many hospitals, clinics, nursing associations, and other organizations offer prenatal classes. These classes usually include exercise and general prenatal instruction for the mother, and some instruction for the father. Often they include a visit to the maternity ward of a local hospital.

The purpose of these classes is not merely to dispel the fear of childbirth. They are also intended to teach the mother (and father) what will happen during birth, and what to expect.

The exercises taught in these classes are aimed at muscle control and breathing control. The benefit of these exercises is that they can give the mother greater muscular control during birth. Greater muscular control can ease the stress of labor. They also improve general muscle tone, which helps the mother regain her figure after the baby is born.

Very few women who are in good health before conception have any difficulty during pregnancy. The forces of nature seem to strive to help the mother and her baby during this important period. After it is over, many women say they have never felt better in their lives.

11

HOW A
BABY IS BORN

For many, many years children have been told all sorts of strange stories about how babies are born. Some children have been told that babies are carried into the world by storks flying at night. Other children believe that a baby is brought to its mother by a doctor in his little black bag. There are also many stories that babies are born through their mother's mouths or belly buttons.

Why have so many strange, untrue stories been told of how a baby is born? It may be that many adults think the *true* story of childbirth is too hard for young people to understand. Actually, it's not that difficult to understand how a baby is born. The birth of a baby is not very complicated; it is a simple but wonderful and exciting process.

A baby is born when it leaves its mother's body. For nine months it grows inside its mother's **uterus**. In time it is ready to be born and live in the outside world.

Childbirth is an exciting experience for the mother, father, and the baby. A woman knows that she has been carrying her baby within her body. But not until he is born can she hold him in her arms and see that she really has a new baby.

While a woman is pregnant, her husband can be only a friendly assistant. After all, it is his wife who is bearing the baby. But on the day the baby is born, the husband is a father. There is now someone new and wonderful in his life.

It is wonderful for the baby to be born because at long last he is on his own. At the moment of birth the baby joins the world of living, working, and loving human beings. He no longer has to live within his mother and be protected by her body. He is born, and begins his life as a separate person.

There is great excitement in a family on the day a baby is born. If it is the first baby in the family, the husband and wife will be happy, but perhaps a little scared. It will be the first time they become parents, and anything done for the first time is a journey into the unknown.

The mother may be the star performer the day she gives birth, but she needs all the friendly help she can get. Her husband must give his wife all the love and understanding he

can when she is having *their* baby. The mother also needs help from her doctor and nurses.

Today most babies are born in hospitals. The doctors and nurses who work in hospitals know a great deal about childbirth and how to make it safe for both the mother and baby.

When will the baby be born

When a doctor tells a woman she is pregnant, usually the first question she asks is, "When will I have my baby?"

Most babies are born about 266 days (9 months) after they were conceived. Very few are born exactly on day 266. Most are born during the two weeks before and after the 266th day.

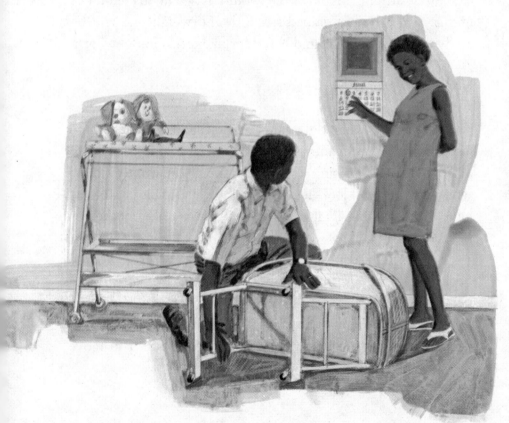

Some babies are born as much as one or two months early. They are premature babies and are sometimes called "premies." Premature babies are small, usually under 5½ pounds, and weak when they are born. They need special hospital care. Although they can perform all of the vital life functions, they are not strong enough to live outside of the uterus without help. A premie lives in a heated incubator crib where he can grow strong, much as he would have in his mother's uterus. When he has gained strength and weight, he will be ready to be taken home and cared for like any other newborn.

Nearing the end of pregnancy

Around day 266 when the mother and father have reached the last weeks of **pregnancy,** every day seems long. They are anxious to see, hold, and love their baby. They want to know what the baby will look like. Will it have curly hair or straight hair? How much will it weigh? Will it look like mother or like father?

By the ninth month of pregnancy the mother is very large because her baby is full size. She is probably tired of carrying her heavy load.

Her baby, too, may be tired of his close quarters. In the early months of pregnancy, he had plenty of room to move

around. He kicked, twisted, stretched, and did somersaults. As the months passed, he grew longer and chubby, and had less room. By the ninth month, he is around 20 inches long and weighs about seven pounds. He is all curled up, with his knees to his chest and his arms tight to his body. There is no more room for acrobatics. When he tries kicking now, the outline of his movements can be seen on his mother's belly.

Childbirth begins

No one knows exactly why childbirth begins. Somehow the uterus, which has been the baby's home for nine months, changes. It no longer holds the baby safe within the mother. Instead, the uterus begins the amazing work of sending the baby into the world.

While the baby grew inside the mother, the wall of her uterus stretched outward. With the baby ready to be born, the

177

uterus stops stretching. It begins to push inward against the baby. This movement is called a *contraction.*

A pregnant woman feels contractions as twinges or slight cramps in her lower back and deep in her abdomen. When an expectant mother feels the first contraction, she knows the time has come for her baby to be born. This part of childbirth is called **labor.** Labor is a very descriptive word, because the mother works hard with each contraction to help her baby be born. The satisfaction of childbirth is her reward.

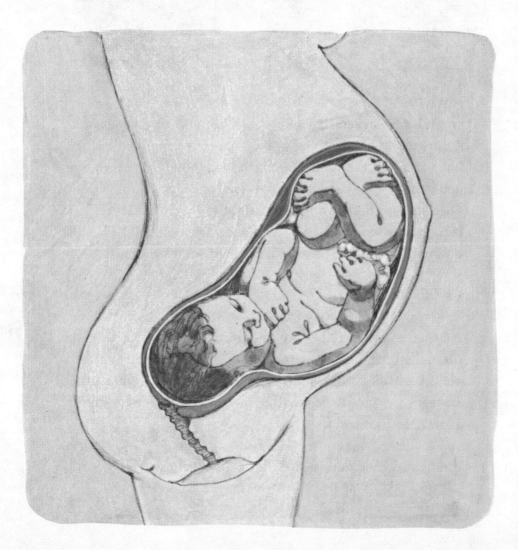

The mother may tell her husband that she thinks her labor has started, and he will phone the doctor to tell him the good news. The doctor will ask how often she is feeling contractions. When they start, contractions come about every half hour. Soon the contractions come more frequently. The doctor will most likely tell the mother to go to the hospital when the contractions are coming about every five or ten minutes. If the woman plans to have her baby at home, the doctor or midwife will come to her to help in the delivery.

Being prepared for labor

An expectant mother should be prepared for that first contraction of labor. She should have a suitcase packed with clothes for the hospital. She should also know what is happening to her body during childbirth.

Having a baby is a tremendous event. Like any other kind of strenuous, physical work, there is an easy way to do it and a hard way. A woman chooses the hard way when she is tired, nervous, jittery, and frightened. If she has not learned or read anything about childbirth, she may feel frightened and nervous. Being frightened can make a little pain hurt a lot.

Childbirth is easy when the mother is not afraid, and understands what is happening to her. She is rested, relaxed, and at ease. Her body is not badly upset by labor cramps. The mother who has an easy time in childbirth is usually the woman who has trained for it.

Training for childbirth is a special way to have a baby. Sometimes this method is called **natural childbirth,** because it helps the mother have her baby in the most natural way possible—that is, without relying much on medication.

179

During pregnancy the mother practices relaxation and breathing exercises which will help her control her body so she can give **birth** with little pain. If there is severe pain, the doctor will give her drugs to ease the discomfort.

In the hospital

When a woman gets to the hospital, she is taken to the labor room. There her doctor examines her to find out how close the baby is to being born. He checks her cervix, the neck of the uterus, and finds out how wide it has opened.

During the first stage of labor the muscles of the uterus are contracting and pulling open the cervix. The cervix stretches like the neck of a sweater when you pull it over your head. The neck of the sweater may be only a few inches around before you slip it over your head. But it can stretch several inches to make room for your head.

The first stage of labor is over when the cervix has stretched open enough for the baby to pass through into the **vagina** (or birth canal). This process usually takes about ten hours, and can become tiresome for the mother. However, there is nothing she can do to hurry it along. She simply must wait for the uterus to do its job. She needs the company of her husband or a friend to help pass the time away. A mother having a baby should never be left alone.

Early in labor there may be a gush of water from the mother's vagina. This is called the breaking of the bag of waters. During prenatal life the baby floated in the warm amniotic sac. When it is time for the baby to be born, there is no need for the water sac. The uterine contractions usually

180   force the sac to break, and the fluids flow out the vagina.

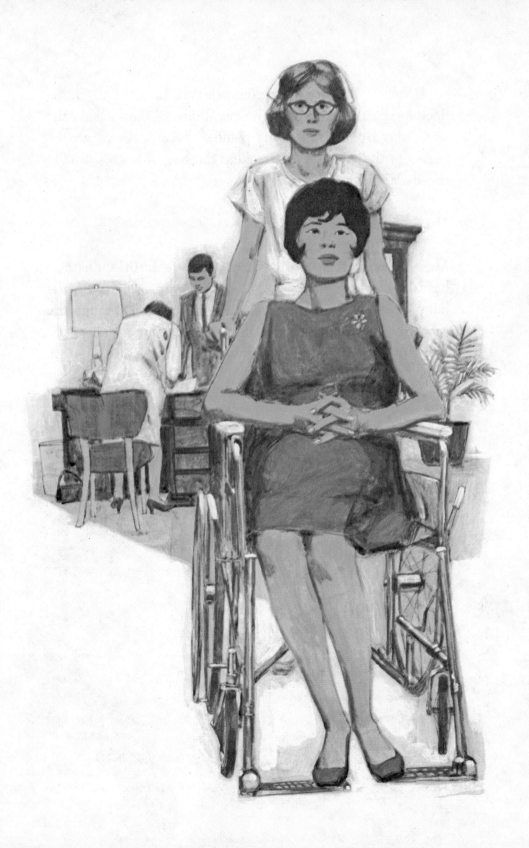

However, if the bag of waters does not break by itself, the doctor makes a small cut in the membrane of the sac, and the water flows out. This cut is painless because there are no nerves in the membrane. Breaking the bag of waters usually speeds labor along.

The baby's head

Most babies rest upside down just before birth, with their heads held snugly in the bottom of the uterus. Therefore, the baby's head is the first part of his body to push through the cervix, or neck of the uterus. If the cervix is too small or the baby too big, the doctor will perform a **Caesarean birth.**

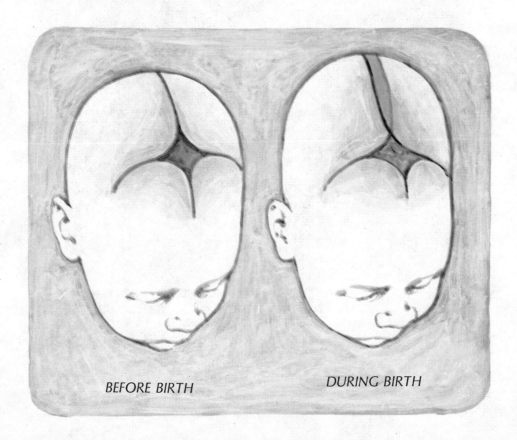

BEFORE BIRTH

DURING BIRTH

It is easiest for a baby to be born head first. The head is the largest solid part of his body, and it is good for it to lead the way out. If a baby is born buttocks or feet first, his birth is called a **breech birth.** A doctor must take extra care with a breech birth.

The baby's skull is not solid bone at birth. There needs to be some give-and-take if it is to pass through the vagina. The skull, a masterpiece of engineering, is made of four pieces of bone attached by connective tissue. It is as if the bones were held together with strong strips of canvas.

When the baby is born, the four pieces of bone are pushed together, and the baby's head gets temporarily out of shape. This temporary shaping of the baby's head at birth is called *molding.* After birth the baby's head gets back into shape, and no longer has a funny peak in the back or a peculiar bump on one side.

In the middle of the baby's head there is a soft spot called the *fontanel.* The fontanel is the place where the four skull bones meet. It takes about two years for this soft spot to become solid bone. You cannot really hurt a baby by touching the fontanel because the brain is protected by a thick membrane.

Second stage of labor

The second stage of labor is much shorter than the first. It is the work of the mother's muscles to push the baby through the vagina into the outside world. By now the mother has been taken into the delivery room and is being attended to by her doctor and a number of nurses.

While the uterus continues to contract, the mother can help in the delivery of her baby. With each contraction the mother pushes down hard with the muscles of her abdomen. Often the pushing feels like a great need to bear down, like the feeling of a bowel movement. Some mothers cannot hold back because their bodies force them to push. The nurse may ask them to pant like a puppy to slow down the pushes. Other mothers must tell themselves to push hard with each contraction so that they help the birth process along.

Cramps in the second stage of labor are strong and come quickly, one after another. The doctor may give the mother some medicine or drugs to ease the pain. Many mothers are so busy pushing that they don't pay much attention to the pain of the contractions and don't need pain relievers.

The doctor must be careful about giving the mother drugs when she is having a baby. The drugs may pass from the mother's body through the **placenta** to the baby. Drugs can make the baby "dopey." All babies should be wide awake at birth, ready to begin a vigorous, healthy new life.

There have been many stories of how painful childbirth can be. In movies and books it has been described as an awful and painful experience for women. Childbirth need not be a terrible experience, and it usually is not. If a woman understands what is happening, and if she has good medical care, her labor and delivery can be easy. Many women say, "Having a baby was the happiest time of my life."

The obstetrician (doctor who delivers babies) does much to make childbirth a happy experience. His most important job is caring for the physical well-being of the mother and child. In addition, his attitude during a birth can help to reassure even the most nervous mother-to-be.

Often an obstetrician will perform an episiotomy during the delivery. An episiotomy is a simple bit of surgery to prevent a woman's tissues from tearing. The doctor may believe that the force of the baby's head will tear the vaginal opening. In order to prevent a tear, he makes a small cut in the skin around the opening. The cut doesn't hurt the mother because the doctor numbs the area with a pain-killing medicine. After the baby is born, the small cut is repaired.

The baby is born

After all the work of labor, the baby is finally born. Slowly his head comes out of the birth canal. The doctor gently holds the baby's head in his hands, and there is a pause. Suddenly, with one or two more pushes, the baby's whole body slithers out. The baby takes his first good breath of air and

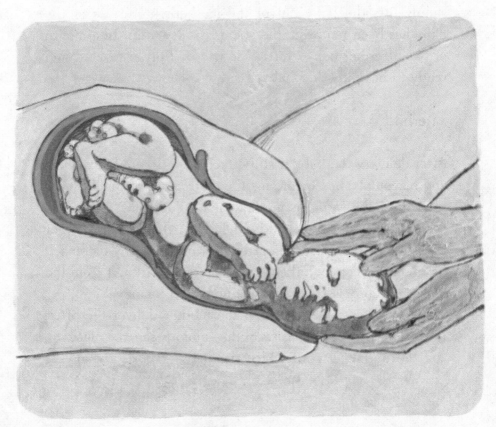

cries. The doctor may give him a small spank to get him started. It is wonderful for a mother to be awake and hear this first cry when her baby is born.

There are times, however, when the mother can't be awake for the birth of her baby. A mother is given an anesthetic and put to sleep if her baby must be delivered by a Caesarean section. A Caesarean section is a major surgical operation that can be done very safely. It is performed when it is not safe for the baby to be born in the usual way through the birth canal. For one reason or another the baby cannot pass easily out of his mother.

When the time comes for her baby to be born, the mother goes to the hospital and is prepared for surgery. The doctor makes a small cut through her **abdomen** and uterine wall. He simply lifts the baby out of the mother's uterus. After the baby has been removed, the opening is sewn up. In a month or two after her baby's birth, she will be fully recovered and ready to have another baby if she wants.

Afterbirth

After delivery the baby is still attached to the umbilical cord and placenta. The doctor cuts the cord and completely separates the baby from his mother for the first time. There are no nerves in the cord, and neither the baby nor his mother feels the cut. A small stump remains on the baby's stomach for about a week, and then it falls off. The mark left from the **umbilical cord** is the baby's belly button, or navel.

The doctor must also help the mother deliver the **afterbirth.** The afterbirth consists of the amniotic sac, the placenta, and the umbilical cord. Once the baby is born, the uterus

keeps contracting, and it shrinks in size. The shrinking forces the tissues of the afterbirth to break away from the uterine wall. With a few pushes the afterbirth is delivered. Sometimes the doctor helps by pressing down on the woman's abdomen.

Normally a woman rests in the hospital for a few days after childbirth. The nurses help her take care of her baby until she goes home.

At last the mother and father have their new baby. They can answer all the questions they have been asking themselves for nine months. It's a boy, or it's a girl. She is dark, or she is fair. They can count his fingers and toes. He's nice to cuddle, and he's good to feel. But most of all they have a child to love.

12

WHAT HAPPENS TO A NEWBORN

A new baby has been born. He has crossed the bridge between two kinds of life. He announced that crossing with a loud cry.

Already he has expressed his own individuality by the strength of that cry and by the ways in which he is different from other babies born in the same hospital on the same day. The doctors and nurses start to keep charts and records because he is now living a life on his own. He is separated from his mother for the first time.

He will depend on his mother for food and care for a long time to come, but he is no longer silent about the care he receives. He can cry and make his wants known. He will soon be able to gurgle or sigh contentedly, expressing satisfaction.

Most babies have been preparing for this moment for nine months. The miracle of **birth** is that most of the time everything goes well, in spite of all the events that happen very quickly to both the mother and the baby.

The drama of arrival

Before birth, the baby was receiving oxygen from the blood carried through the **umbilical cord** from the **placenta.** His lungs were formed and growing, and were even occasionally moving. But they were not doing their intended jobs. They were not taking oxygen from the air and adding it to the blood, or removing carbon dioxide from the blood and exhaling it.

At the time of birth, the oxygen supply from the placenta is cut off. The body is alerted that the time has come for the lungs to take over on their own.

A change in the heart is also triggered. Until this time, blood has entered the body through the umbilical cord, circulated through the baby's body, while losing oxygen and gaining carbon dioxide, and then back out through the umbilical cord.

When birth approaches, a special opening in the heart closes so that blood will go from the heart to the lungs, where it exchanges carbon dioxide for oxygen, back to the heart, and then through the body.

When the baby is born, he is ready to start breathing. The doctor will immediately hold him upside down and clean

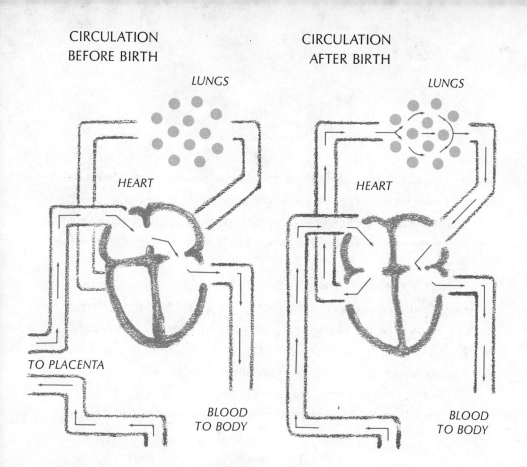

LUNGS

LUNGS

HEART

HEART

TO PLACENTA

BLOOD
TO BODY

BLOOD
TO BODY

out his nose and throat passages. He may give the baby a spank to stimulate the lungs into taking over their job. The baby lets out a cry that gets its diaphragm moving, doing the job of making the lungs work which it will do for the rest of the new being's life.

Doctors are not absolutely certain just what makes the lungs start to work. It could be the change in pressure from the mother's **uterus** to the outside world that sets the diaphragm moving. It may be that the excess of carbon dioxide that accumulates in the baby's diaphragm in the few moments before birth somehow triggers the vital change.

191

During birth, a baby goes through a complete change of environment in just a few minutes. Never again will he go through such a dramatic change so quickly. Before birth he was floating in a pool of liquid, and was weightless. Now he feels the forces of gravity and air pressure. He feels the touch of blankets and of people's hands. After months of darkness, he suddenly sees bright lights. Harsh sounds come from all directions.

After the doctor is sure the baby is breathing properly, he puts a clamp on the umbilical cord about two inches from the baby's belly. He ties a thread tightly around the cord, then cuts the cord. This doesn't hurt the baby because there are no nerve endings in the umbilical cord.

Now the baby is a completely separate being. He is no longer linked to his mother. In about ten days, the stub of

cord will dry up and drop off. Only the scar of the **navel,** also called "belly button," will remain to show that there was once a physical connection between him and his mother.

Before the baby can rest from the experience he has gone through, more things must be done. The doctor will clean the baby, gently wiping fluid and mucus from his eyes, nose, and body creases. Then he will put a few drops of silver nitrate in the baby's eyes. This is required by law. Many years ago, babies frequently went blind from infections acquired during birth. Silver nitrate kills any possible infection without hurting the baby's eyes.

A new baby is a legal person. He has rights and individuality. In large hospitals where many babies are born every day, it is important to be sure there is no chance of mixing up babies and mothers. Therefore, right after birth, before baby or mother leave the delivery room, some doctors make a record in ink of the baby's footprints. These footprints will never change throughout life, and may someday serve as a means of identification.

The doctor will also probably put a tiny bracelet of plastic beads or a plastic band around the baby's wrist with his family name on it. The mother will wear an identical bracelet. The bracelets will stay in place until the mother leaves the hospital with her own baby.

Having made sure that the baby is breathing properly, that his eyesight is protected, and that he won't get mixed up with another baby, the doctor then shows the baby to the mother. She may be very tired, but she wants to know that her baby is all right. She wants to know if it is a boy or a girl. Does it have the right number of fingers and toes? Can she tell who it will look like?

Then the baby is placed in a warm bassinette, with his head lower than his legs to help him breathe. Now he has a chance to recover from the events he has gone through, and to begin to investigate the big world he has entered.

What is the newborn baby like?

While the new mother relaxes from the excitement of delivery and the father celebrates the birth of his child, the baby is being carefully examined by a doctor.

The newborn baby is a squalling red bundle. He is shaped very much like a human being. He has a head—a large one—two arms, and two legs. He is like other human babies—yet very unlike any other.

He has probably spent 38 to 40 weeks growing and is called a **full-term baby.** He weighs about 7 pounds. If a boy, he probably weighs about half a pound more than a girl baby. If he's the second or third child in a family, he may weigh more than his oldest sister or brother did at birth. He is probably 19 or 20 inches long, if the doctor can get him to lie flat to be measured.

Sometimes a baby is born before it is full term. Such a birth is called a **premature birth.** It is usually difficult for a doctor or mother to figure exactly when full term is, so any

baby that weighs less than 5½ pounds is considered premature. He needs special care and feeding and extra warmth
to help him through the first days.

A premature baby is usually kept for a while in an **incubator.** This is an enclosed, heated bassinette. An incubator is
more like the mother's womb than a regular bassinette. An
incubator keeps the baby warm and moistens his breathing
passages. It can provide extra oxygen if the baby needs help
in breathing. The hours or days a baby spends in an incubator give him a better chance to complete his development
and to adjust to life in the outside world.

Whether premature or full-term, the newborn baby may
seem to have too large a head to fit his body. The baby's
large head is the most important sign of his being a very

special mammal. Most other mammals grow in the womb until they are much more mature and more ready to tackle independent life.

An infant seal, for example, must be ready to plunge into icy sea water. Seals spend about 350 days in the womb and are ready to swim soon after birth. A baby horse must be able to run when danger threatens. A baby horse can run soon after birth, but he spends about 335 days in the womb.

A human being, however, differs from all other mammals in his great intelligence. Great intelligence requires a large brain, and a large brain requires a large head.

However, there is a limit to how large a head can be and still get through the birth passage of a human mother. So during the long process of man's evolution, a trade was made. After only about 266 days, human babies have heads that are comparatively larger than many mammals. But they are born more helpless. They need a longer time of parental care.

The baby may have soft, downy, dark hair covering his large head. He may even have hair on his shoulders or face. This hair will fall out during the first weeks after birth and not be replaced until regular hair-growing time later. Once in a while, a baby is born with a few tiny teeth. These, too, will fall out, not to be replaced until later.

The baby will probably have grayish-blue eyes which can later turn to blue or brown. When he cries, no tears come from his eyes, and won't for another few weeks.

His eyes are open, and he seems to see, but he can't really focus on anything yet. He can, however, see movement, colors, and shapes. Gradually during the next few weeks, his eyes will begin to focus on his mother and on certain movements that mean something to him.

At first, the baby has a grayish, greasy coating, called the **vernix,** on his skin. This coating protected the baby's skin before birth. The vernix is washed off the baby's skin shortly after he is born. Underneath, the baby's skin is velvety soft, softer than it will ever be again, because he has spent nine months floating in a soft, soothing fluid.

The new baby has little control of his muscles, but he can make some movements. These movements will usually be made by his whole body instead of a single arm or leg. However, he can turn his head from side to side. If the doctor holds him upright with his feet on a firm surface, he will make walking movements with his legs. His tiny fingers can grasp something quite firmly.

Some of the newborn's movements are reflexive, or automatic. The baby doesn't need to learn them, because they are natural abilities. One of these movements is sucking. When the doctor touches a newborn's lips, the baby starts sucking.

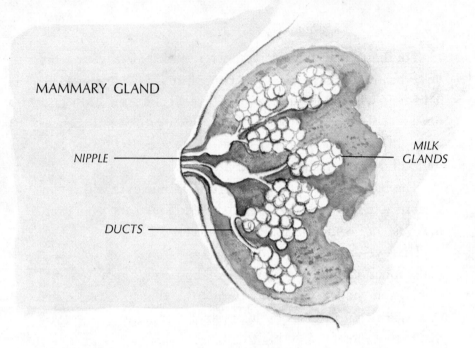

MAMMARY GLAND

NIPPLE

MILK GLANDS

DUCTS

When the doctor touches a cheek, the baby's head automatically turns to that side. This "rooting" reflex, and the sucking reflex, will be very important when the baby is taken to his mother for feeding for the first time.

The baby also has a "startle" reflex. Whenever his position is changed suddenly, his whole body will contract in a spasm. The doctor can tell from the startle reflex whether the newborn's muscles are functioning properly.

Feeding the newborn

The newborn baby does not eat right away. This waiting to eat will make the baby lose some of his birth weight, perhaps seven to ten per cent of it. Once he is on milk, however, he regains that weight very quickly.

The glands in the mother's breasts do not begin to produce milk until three or four days after the baby is born. The

198

hormones in her body need to adjust from a pregnant condition to a milk-producing, non-pregnant condition.

If the mother is going to feed her baby with her own milk, a nurse will bring the baby to her about eight to 12 hours after he is born. As she holds the baby, the touch of her breast on his cheek makes him turn his head. The nipple touches his lips, and he begins to suck. Although there is no milk, the breasts contain a whitish fluid called **colostrum.**

Colostrum supplies three main benefits for the baby. First, it provides nourishment for the baby until his mother's breasts produce milk. Second, it stimulates the intestinal tract, and causes the baby to get rid of some accumulated matter from his bowels. Third, it appears to give the child some antibodies he needs for protection from disease. Before the baby was born, he built up a supply of antibodies from his mother's blood. This supply lasts about four to six months, and is reinforced by the antibodies from the colostrum. Later, the baby's body will start to build up its own disease fighters.

Sucking by the baby on the mother's breast stimulates her glands to produce milk. Even though the baby is not being fed milk during his first two or three days, his visits to his mother's breast get her ready to produce milk.

These visits also do a very important job in letting the infant get to know his mother's touch and feel and smell. They assure him that he is loved, and that gentle hands are taking care of him. For nine months he has been in constant touch with his mother, in the most life-giving way possible. Now he is in a new world. The love of his mother relieves the anxieties of coping with that new world.

Many mothers, for one reason or another, do not want to or are unable to nurse their babies at their own breasts. The new baby can be fed just as well from a bottle with a special formula that resembles his mother's milk. A baby fed this way usually grows up just as healthy as a breast-fed baby, provided his mother takes the time to hold, fondle, and love him.

Whether being fed at the breast or from a bottle, the newborn's first learning experiences will come with feeding. He gets to know the feeling of hunger, and he cries lustily because it hurts. He feels the satisfaction of being picked up and fed, and he gets to know the drowsy comfort of then drifting back to sleep.

A newborn baby sleeps much of the time, though the sleeping pattern varies with each baby. This is one of the first signs of individual differences in babies.

The periods when he is awake are not periods of thinking and doing as they will be when he is older. But even in the five or six days in the hospital, this, too, begins to change. The mother begins to notice slight differences in the way he cries. He may seem to stare at her for a moment when feeding, as if to say, "I know this shape and touch. It is the person who feeds me and makes me feel comfortable."

He may take on a regular schedule of demanding food and then sleeping. He begins to react to different sounds in different ways. The gentle rhythm of a lullaby makes him feel secure and sleepy. A sharp noise makes him contract his muscles in sudden tension. He begins to show how long he takes to relax after tension or hunger.

All in all, the tiny infant who looks so much like others at birth begins very quickly to take on a personality, to be

"humanized." The nurses know him as the one who cries so much, or the one who is so patient about being fed on a hospital schedule, or the one who seems to react more to sounds and sights than the little girl in the next bassinette.

If the baby is a boy, his parents may decide to have him circumcised before leaving the hospital. **Circumcision** is the removal of the foreskin of the penis. Centuries ago, it was done as an initiation ceremony into manhood. Today, it is done primarily for reasons of hygiene. The penis is easier to keep clean when it doesn't have the small fold of skin under which bacteria can grow.

Circumcision is often done on the fourth or fifth day, just before the mother and baby leave the hospital. It can be done easily, and the small wound heals very quickly. For members of the Jewish faith, circumcision is a religious ritual which has to be carried out in a specific way. Jewish mothers usually bring their babies back to the hospital when eight days old, and the ritual is performed according to religious rules in a special room of the hospital.

The birth certificate

As soon as a baby is born, he becomes a legal person in his own right. The hospital—or the doctor if the baby is born at home—has the legal responsibility to register the birth of the baby with the local government. The **birth certificate** that is filed will always be proof of when and where he was born.

The standard birth certificate consists of two parts. The top part contains the name the parents have decided to give the baby, the date and time of its birth, the place of birth, and whether the baby is a boy or girl. This part also contains information about the address and age of the mother and father, and a place for the doctor to sign, verifying the information. This is the part of the certificate that you would usually get if you asked for a copy of your birth certificate.

The certificate's bottom part is not usually sent when a birth certificate is requested. This part has information about the parents' race, educational level, whether or not the baby was born of parents who were married, the kind of care the mother had before the baby was born, the weight at birth, other children in the family, and other things. This information is kept secret. This information is used by federal and state governments to find out how the population is changing, and whether war or economic changes affect the population as a whole. It is used to find out whether people are getting married and having babies at an earlier or later age.

To the mother and father who are taking a new baby home from the hospital, that baby is not a statistic. He is a new being, whom they, in their love, have given life. He is somewhat like other babies, but he is uniquely himself. He can learn, and he will go on learning the rest of his life. He needs loving care, and will soon be able to let his parents know that he returns their love. He moves and explores the world with increasing interest. Gradually, as he grows, the traits and abilities he inherited from his parents will be mixed with the characteristics and skills that he learns just by being himself. Finally, as a grown man or woman, he will probably experience birth again—but this time as a parent.

13

WHO WILL THE BABY BE LIKE

Every day in the year, about 190,000 babies are born in the world. All have tiny faces and usually the same number of ears, fingers, arms, legs, and toes. All are little humans, quite alike in size, and with the same needs for food, love, protection, and learning. Each also has his or her own special features. Each is like every other baby and also unlike any other baby born on that day, or on any other day in history.

If these same 190,000 people were to meet on their 25th birthday, their specialness would be even more obvious than at birth. Some would be very tall, some very short, and the rest would be somewhere in between. They would vary from very fat to very thin. Skin colors would be yellow, brown, white, reddish, and all kinds of shades in between. There would be great differences in hair and eye colorings.

Equally different would be the many types of personalities, mental abilities, talents, and ways of living in these 190,000 people. All were born on the same day and were similar in many ways. Within 25 years, each had grown into an individual who is like other human beings, but who is also different from other humans.

Scientists who study human characteristics do not know all of the reasons for the differences and similarities in this group, or in any other group of people. Today, however, they believe that the two strongest forces which influence human life are **heredity** and **environment.**

Heredity and environment

Heredity is a word used to mean the way in which certain characteristics are passed from parents to children, generation after generation. Because of heredity, each baby is born with human characteristics which make him like, as well as unlike, other people.

The force of heredity begins acting long before birth. It creates a pattern of characteristics which almost always remains unchanged throughout a person's life. Some of these characteristics, called *inherited characteristics*, are skin color, bone structure, and sex.

Environment is a word used to stand for all the conditions which are part of a person's life and affect his development. Included in a person's environment are the foods he eats, the home he is brought up in, the diseases he may have, and the

206

ideas, people, and education he is exposed to. The characteristics acquired through environment are called *acquired characteristics,* and include a person's religious beliefs, prejudices,
and style of living.

Throughout life the two forces of heredity and environment shape and form each person's physical appearance,
intelligence, and personality.

One example of the forces of heredity and environment
can be seen in the way babies learn to talk. Because all babies
inherit human characteristics, all make similar babbles, coos,
laughs, and cries. They do not mew like kittens or chirp like
birds. They all sound surprisingly alike—like human babies—
no matter which country they are born in. In this particular
characteristic, their heredity is the same.

Their environments, however, are vastly different. As they
begin to say their first words, they speak the language of their

207

parents and others around them. A French child begins speaking French, a Chinese baby learns Chinese, and a baby born in the United States learns American English.

Why is it that some people have black skin and others have a yellowish tint? Why are certain people blonde, blue-eyed, and tall, and others are dark, brown-eyed, and short? Why do some men become great baseball players, and others never learn to hit the ball? Why do some people become well-known artists, writers, or musicians, and others never achieve fame at all?

The key to some of these questions can be found in heredity, others in environment. Most answers, however, are found in both heredity and environment.

How does heredity work?

For many centuries, people wondered why certain traits seemed to "run in families." They thought of all sorts of reasons, but none gave the true answer.

In the 19th century, an Austrian monk named Gregor Mendel began to understand the mystery of heredity. Working with pea plants, he discovered that characteristics passed from one generation to another in a regular, orderly way. He felt that something caused traits from parent plants to reappear in new seedlings, but he did not understand what that "something" was.

In the 20th century, scientists finally found out what that something was. With the help of high-powered microscopes, they were able to study the **cell,** the basic unit of all life. They could now understand some things about heredity that had been hidden in the tiny particles of cells for centuries.

Each cell is made up of three main parts—the *nucleus* (which controls the actions of the cell), *cytoplasm* (living matter surrounding the nucleus), and a *membrane* (outer covering). All perform functions which are necessary for life. Scientists discovered that **chromosomes** in the nucleus of the cell held the key to an understanding of heredity.

Chromosomes are like tiny strands of beads. They occur in pairs. (For each chromosome, there is another one which looks exactly like it.) Every living thing has a specific number of chromosome pairs in each of its cells. A cell in a rabbit, for example, has 22 chromosomes (11 pairs), corn cells have 20 (10 pairs), and a pea plant cell has 14 (7 pairs). Human cells have 46 chromosomes (23 pairs).

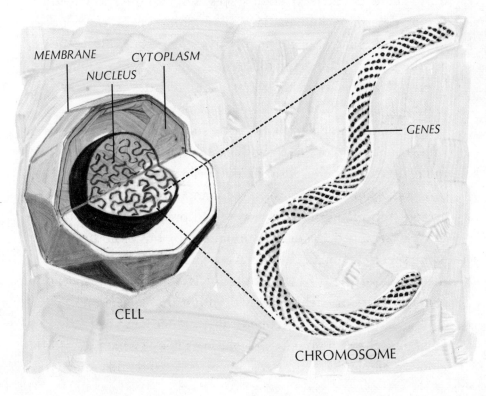

MEMBRANE CYTOPLASM

NUCLEUS

GENES

CELL

CHROMOSOME

Each chromosome is made up of many **genes,** tiny chemicals which determine heredity. Genes are arranged in a very orderly way in chromosomes, like beads on a necklace. There can be hundreds or even thousands of genes in one chromosome.

From their location in the chromosomes of all cells, genes cause the development of physical characteristics throughout the body. They control each cell, causing it to produce whatever characteristic the genes have blueprinted for that cell. Genes determine the size of ears and noses, shapes of eyes, colors of hair, and many other traits.

Some genes by themselves can cause a specific trait to develop. Others need the help of other genes to determine a trait. There are at least eight genes, for example, which together determine human skin color. Since genes can work together in millions of different ways, these skin color genes are the cause of the many different shades of colors found in human skin. For very important characteristics, such as sex and body build, hundreds of genes work together.

Genes are made up of a fantastic substance, called *DeoxyriboNucleic Acid,* or DNA (with each letter pronounced separately). DNA is believed to be the basic substance of all life. It is made up of many chemical compounds which can be arranged in many different ways. The precise way in which DNA is arranged in genes determines: 1) the basic traits of every species (human babies have human characteristics—not the characteristics of plants or animals); and 2) the special characteristics of each individual within that species.

Each time body cells divide to produce new cells, they must give the same number of chromosomes (which also includes genes and DNA), to each new cell. To do this, they go through a process called **mitosis.** During mitosis, the chromosomes double themselves. When the cell splits, the exact same number and type of chromosomes goes to each new "half."

How does heredity pass to a new baby?

So that each new baby will have 46 chromosomes in each of its cells, nature has created a special type of cell division for reproductive cells, the sperm and egg. This process, called **meiosis,** leaves each sperm and egg cell with only *half* the number of chromosomes, or 23. When a sperm and egg join during fertilization, together they make up the 46 chromosomes necessary to begin the life of a new baby.

During meiosis egg and sperm cells split *without* doubling their chromosomes. Also, some of the genes in the chromosomes rearrange themselves in a new way within the chromosomes. When meiosis is complete, each new sperm or egg cell has a different combination of chromosomes from the parent cell which formed it.

When fertilization occurs, a sperm from the father unites with the egg from the mother, and their chromosomes pair up with each other. The new cell, which will eventually develop into a new baby, gets half of its chromosomes from the father and half from the mother. Each baby receives half of his or her heredity from the father and half from the mother.

There are more than eight million different ways that a sperm and egg can unite together during fertilization. Therefore, parents can give many different hereditary combinations to each of their children. Some brothers and sisters may receive quite similar hereditary gifts and be very much alike. Others may be different from each other in many ways.

HOW CHROMOSOMES PASS TO NEW CELLS

(SIMPLIFIED ILLUSTRATIONS)

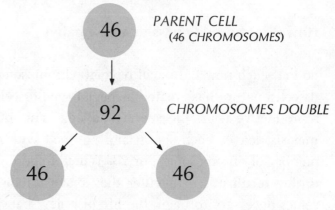

MITOSIS (BODY CELLS)

46   *PARENT CELL* (46 CHROMOSOMES)

92   *CHROMOSOMES DOUBLE*

46   46

NEW BODY CELLS (46 CHROMOSOMES EACH)

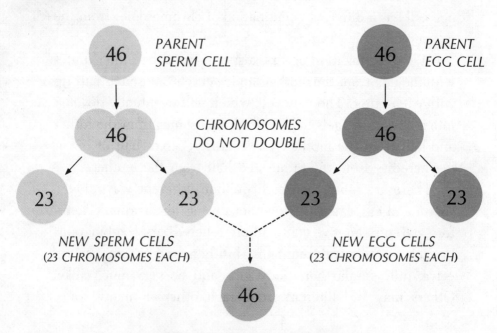

MEIOSIS (REPRODUCTIVE CELLS)

46   *PARENT SPERM CELL*   46   *PARENT EGG CELL*

46   *CHROMOSOMES DO NOT DOUBLE*   46

23   23   23   23

NEW SPERM CELLS (23 CHROMOSOMES EACH)   *NEW EGG CELLS* (23 CHROMOSOMES EACH)

46

FERTILIZED EGG CELL (46 CHROMOSOMES)

One important reason why children from one set of parents may be different from one another is that some genes are stronger in determining heredity than others.

Strong genes are called *dominant genes*. When a dominant gene meets with a weaker gene, the stronger dominates —it decides what characteristics will develop. A weaker gene, called a *recessive gene* can only dictate heredity when it pairs with the same type of recessive gene during fertilization.

Some dominant genes are those for black hair, curly hair, and dimpled cheeks. The corresponding recessive genes are for blonde hair, straight hair, and smooth cheeks. If the father's chromosomes have genes for black, curly hair, and dimpled cheeks, and the mother's chromosomes have genes for blonde, straight hair, and smooth cheeks, the baby will probably have black, curly hair, and dimpled cheeks.

If, during another time of conception, the fertilizing sperm carries genes for the recessive traits (and the egg also has the same genes), the second baby will probably have blonde, straight hair, and smooth cheeks. A recessive gene remains "hidden" in the chromosomes of a person throughout life.

The general dominant-recessive rule of heredity is *not* an always-to-be-followed rule, however. Many times, characteristics are influenced mostly by dominant genes, but are also affected by recessive genes. With the parents described above, one child might have brown, partly-curly hair, and one dimpled cheek.

At the moment of fertilization, each baby receives his own set of chromosomes for characteristics and development. The genes in these chromosomes and his environment affect his rate of growth, distinct physical appearance, and many other special characteristics that are his alone.

213

HEREDITY OF HAIR COLOR

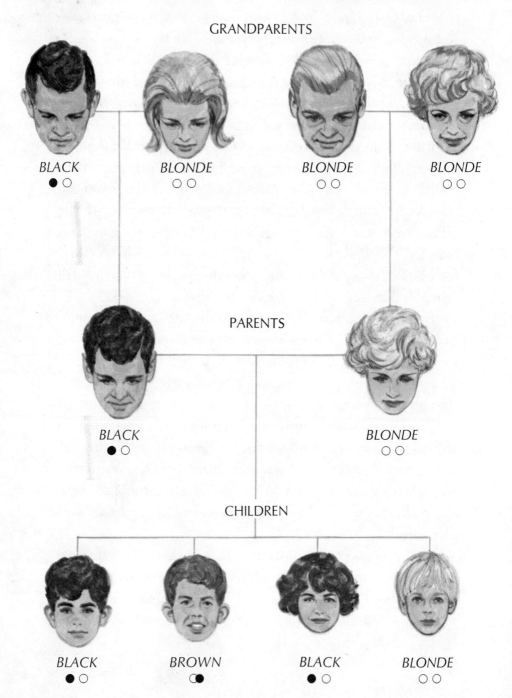

● GENE FOR BLACK HAIR   ○ GENE FOR BLONDE HAIR

GRANDPARENTS

BLACK
● ○

BLONDE
○ ○

BLONDE
○ ○

BLONDE
○ ○

PARENTS

BLACK
● ○

BLONDE
○ ○

CHILDREN

BLACK
● ○

BROWN
◑

BLACK
● ○

BLONDE
○ ○

The only exception to this "specialness" is found in identical multiple births, such as twins or triplets. Since identical twins develop from the same sperm and egg, they both inherit the exact same hereditary characteristics.

Sex determination

One very important characteristic that is set at the time of fertilization is a baby's sex. There is one pair of chromosomes in the cells of a person's body which control male or female traits. These "sex chromosomes" are named "Y" for male and "X" for female. (These letters are *only* for the purpose of identification.)

All of the cells in a woman's body have an XX pattern of chromosomes. When her egg cells divide in meiosis, each new cell has one X chromosome. All of the cells in a man's body have an XY pattern. When his sperm are produced, half of the new cells have an X and half have a Y sex chromosome.

If a Y sperm fertilizes the egg, the sex chromosome pair will be XY, and the baby will be a boy. If an X sperm fertilizes the egg, the new chromosome pair will be XX, and the baby will be a girl.

Defective genes

Considering all that genes do within the human body, it is quite surprising that they seldom make mistakes. Unfortunately, however, something does occasionally go wrong within a gene, and a baby may then inherit a defect or disease.

Certain forms of deafness and blindness can be inherited. Harelip, club foot, cleft palate, having six fingers or toes, or

IF YOU CANNOT SEE THE COLORED SYMBOLS IN THE SQUARES BELOW, YOU MAY HAVE A COLOR VISION DEFECT.

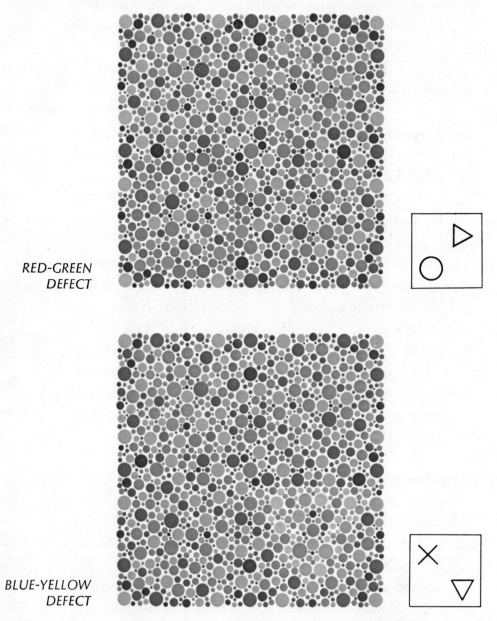

RED-GREEN DEFECT

BLUE-YELLOW DEFECT

216

These reproductions illustrate only the composition of color test plates. Due to color deviations in color processes they are not valid tests for color vision deficiences. Reprinted courtesy American Optical Corporation.

being a midget can also result from heredity. Some forms of mental defects or retardation may possibly result from defective genes or chromosomes. One form of inherited mental retardation is mongolism, also called Down's syndrome. Children with Down's syndrome have 47 chromosomes, not the normal 46. This retards them mentally, and also changes their physical appearance to some degree.

Some inherited defects are called "sex-linked" defects. These are normally carried (hidden) in the X chromosome of a woman. The defect does not affect her, but it may affect her sons. Two sex-linked defects are hemophilia and color blindness. Hemophilia is a serious condition in which the child's blood is unable to clot properly. If a hemophiliac person is cut, even slightly, it is extremely difficult to stop the bleeding, and he may bleed to death. Color blindness prevents people from being able to distinguish certain colors. Most color-blind people cannot "see" red or green.

The above diseases and defects, and others that are inherited, are very rare compared to all other traits passed through heredity. It is considered possible that someday defective heredity may be prevented.

Heredity and environment together

In addition to physical traits that are inherited, certain other characteristics may be inherited. Some scientists feel that intelligence is an inherited characteristic, and that talents can also be inherited. The specific genes for these particular traits have never been discovered, however, and it is not really known if these traits are inherited. Until a "music gene" or a "writing gene" is discovered, the answer will be in doubt.

217

It is known that no one can be intelligent, a good mechanic, a fine artist, or a successful musician without a great deal of work. Part of what makes a person intelligent or successful is study, practice, and determination. The environment a person grows up in is very important in determining the attitude he develops towards certain activities. If he is encouraged to try to develop certain abilities, he is much more likely to do so.

If parents try to encourage their children, it does not necessarily follow that their children will be successful. If one or both parents are extremely capable in a particular talent or job, this does not mean that the child will inherit the same capability. It is also true that if a parent is an alcoholic, suffers from mental illness, or is unable to get along well with others, the child will not necessarily inherit any of these characteristics. In all of these cases, the characteristics were most likely acquired by the parents—*not* passed to them through their genes. The same is true for their children.

Without a good environment, many people do not achieve all that they could. A boy may inherit genes for tallness, but if he has a serious disease or a poor diet, his growth may be stunted. A girl may be born with the possibility for great intelligence. If she is unable to get a good education, or is not stimulated at home, she may actually appear to be stupid.

A person's choice

Heredity and environment do not determine *all* of a person's characteristics. Certainly, both have a great deal to do with what a person becomes. There is another factor which is also important, and understanding it can change your life.

That factor is a person's ability to change some important conditions. This ability enables a person to improve on what heredity and environment "give." A young girl may feel that she is "fat and ugly" because of her hereditary body build. Later, she learns how to apply make up, to eat a well-balanced diet, and to exercise. She greatly improves her appearance and her success with other people. A young boy may refuse to study because he believes that he is stupid. Later, he discovers that he is not stupid but that he is lazy. He begins to try to overcome his laziness, and he greatly improves his grades and his chances for future success.

There are many true success stories about people who have had either a poor hereditary or a poor environmental background. Many were born with a physical handicap, or had a very poor family background. Yet, these people refused to let their problems stop them. They found ways to overcome their difficulties.

These people and many others are a reminder that no one is set for life because of heredity or environment. Each person has the ability to bring about changes in his or her life.

14

HOW
YOU GREW

One of the most important parts of your life is the part you probably can't remember—the first few years.

By the time a child is five or six years old, it is fairly clear whether he will be healthy or sickly, and how he will get along with other people. Of course, there is still plenty of room for growth, learning, and change. But the child will never grow so fast, learn so much, or change so deeply as he will during his first years.

When a new baby comes home to join his family, he weighs about seven pounds, and is about 20 inches long. He does not look like a "person," with his tiny, wrinkled body and his funny puffy face. His older brothers and sisters may be disappointed at how helpless and uninteresting he is. They expected a cute, cuddly baby they could play with. Instead, the new baby is not very pretty, and he seems to do nothing but cry, eat, and sleep.

The new baby seems too small to play with, but he is really growing at a rapid rate. After a few weeks he will begin gaining weight steadily—about a pound a month for the first five or six months. At five months he may be twice his birth weight. Then his growth slows down. If it didn't, he would weigh almost a thousand pounds by the time he was three!

NORMAL WEIGHT GAIN FOR TWO BABIES

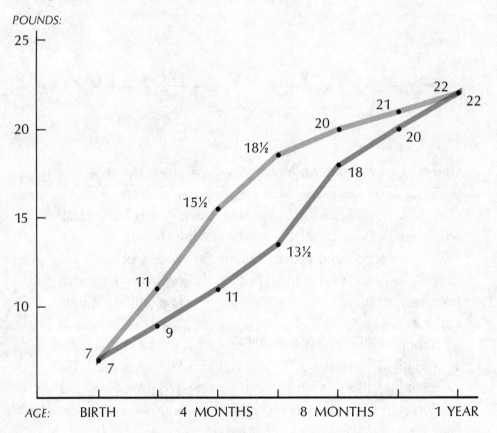

Each baby has his own pattern of growth. No two babies grow at exactly the same rate. One may gain weight rapidly at first and then slow down. Another baby's weight may seem to stand still forever, and then suddenly shoot up. The pound-a-month figure is the average weight gain for newborns.

The average height gain for babies is about ten inches in their first year of life. They grow from a birth measurement of about 20 inches to about 30 inches at age one. After the first birthday, a baby increases in height at a slower rate.

During his first year, a baby grows taller mainly because his torso grows longer. After age one, much of his childhood growth will be in his legs. On the average, a child has reached close to half his adult height by age two.

The newborn's instincts

While a new baby grows, he actually does more than eat, cry, and sleep. If his brothers and sisters watch him closely, they will see that he twitches, sneezes, hiccups, blinks, yawns, kicks, and waves his hands and feet. But he doesn't do these things on purpose. He is not yet able to control most of his body movements.

At first, the only part of his body that he can control is his mouth. A baby is born with the "sucking instinct." Knowing how to suck is very important for newborns because it is their only way of eating.

When a new baby is hungry, he cries. Knowing how to cry is another instinct. When a newborn cries, he screams with what appears to us to be fear and rage. He squirms, kicks, and turns red in the face. Gradually, he learns that hunger goes away; that when he is hungry, he gets fed.

223

The baby also cries when he is uncomfortable, wet, or afraid. Sometimes he cries after he has been fed. That usually means a stomach-ache. At other times he seems to cry just to try out his voice. After all, crying is his only way of talking.

A baby can learn

For many weeks a baby is almost totally helpless, much more helpless than most baby animals. Animals are born with many complex instincts that help them survive. They know how to catch food, whether to hibernate or fly south in the winter, and when and how to mate.

A human baby is born with only a few simple instincts, and he knows practically nothing. He develops more slowly than an animal baby. But by the time he is four years old, the human baby is smarter than the smartest animal.

A human baby is smarter because he has a miraculous brain. His brain gives him the power to reason, to "stop and think" instead of acting on instinct. With each experience he has, his brain develops and his ability to learn increases. Everything he learns from each new experience is stored in his brain for future use.

One of the first pleasurable experiences a baby has is snuggling close to his mother and sucking milk from a bottle or from her breast. Even when he sleeps, he often seems to be dreaming about eating—his mouth makes sucking movements.

If a baby's cries are answered and he can suck milk every few hours, he starts to learn that he is not totally helpless after all. He learns that he can make things happen.

As a baby learns, his brain grows. It actually doubles in size his first year of life. His other body organs grow, too. His

lungs increase in size as he takes deeper and deeper breaths. Also, his breathing rate slows down. Newborn babies all breathe in short, fast puffs.

The pulse of a newborn is much faster than that of an adult. While the baby grew in his mother's body, his pulse was over 100 beats per minute. After a baby is born, his heart keeps developing. His heartbeat slows down and approaches the average for adults of 72 beats per minute.

A baby needs love

For a baby to grow normally, he must be fed when he is hungry, and kept dry and warm. We have learned that there is also something else a baby must have. Scientists who have experimented with baby animals have called it "body contact." Doctors who study human babies often call it "mothering" or "cuddling." We might just call it love.

225

Whatever it is, we have discovered that without it animals become sick and grow up unable to be normal mates and parents. Without it, babies waste away.

Everyone has seen a mother dog, cat, or mouse with her new babies. She spends a great deal of time licking them. Many people believed this licking was only to keep them clean. However, when baby mice were raised in a laboratory without this licking—even though they were kept clean and well fed—they died or failed to grow properly. But when people in the lab stroked the baby mice, the mice thrived.

In many similar experiments, scientists have found that other animals, such as monkeys, need close body contact with a mother—even a make-believe mother. Many scientists believe this contact is also necessary for human babies.

Mammals give their babies body contact when they feed them. All female mammals have special milk glands. Baby

animals spend most of their first days or weeks snuggled up against mother's body, eating and sleeping. Most human mothers feed their babies breast milk, too. Only in a few countries, such as the United States, are many babies fed with cow's milk or formula from a bottle.

Most experts believe that breast feeding is better for the baby—but only if the mother wants to do it. Breast feeding is good for the mother's body and saves her hours of work preparing bottles. When a mother breast feeds, she and no one else must hold the baby and feed him. Breast feeding is good for the baby because the milk is safe and pure. Breast feeding also gives him the cuddling he needs. However, millions of babies have been bottle fed and grew up normally. They still got the cuddling and mothering they needed to grow.

A baby notices the world

If the baby is loved and his physical needs are met, his body and mind will thrive. A baby's mind is always growing. He begins to notice sights, smells, sounds, tastes, and feelings of the world around him.

The baby's hunger for food changes into hunger for experience. He begins to use his body to satisfy this hunger by exploring his surroundings.

227

He starts by using his eyes. When the baby nurses, he watches his mother's face. Soon he associates the delicious feeling of nursing with that face. One day, around the time he's a month or two old, he smiles at that face. And, of course, the face smiles back. Later he will laugh and gurgle when he sees his mother, and cry when she leaves him. He is beginning to express love in a way common only to babies.

He stares at other faces and other objects. Bright lights and pictures on the wall fascinate him. He will follow moving objects with his eyes, holding up his wobbly head for a few minutes before it flops down again. After a few months, he can hold his head up and turn it around. He can see colors and shapes. He reaches out with his eyes for the things and people he loves. Soon he will reach out with his hands.

He spends the next few months getting to know his hands and making them work. First he can reach out and touch a toy, his bottle, or his mother's face. He should be allowed to

touch many different objects in order to learn. He can grab things and bring them to his mouth. He plays with his hands, his feet—anything he can get hold of.

At first, he doesn't use his thumb when he grabs something. He just wraps his whole hand around the object, like a paw. Then, as the months go by, he develops the ability to use four fingers and a thumb. Each time he handles something he can make his fingers work better. He is able to pick things up and drop them again. He can poke and stroke with one finger.

Now, the baby can do a few things for himself. He can explore what is in reach of his mouth, eyes, and hands. He can hold his own bottle, and feed himself a cookie. His next big project is learning to move his whole body by himself.

Learning to move

Most babies are born with relatively large heads, long torsos, and short arms and legs. They usually have short necks and high shoulders. As they get older, their skeletons grow. Their heads no longer seem so large, compared to their bodies. Their necks get longer, their round chests broaden and flatten out, and their arms and legs grow.

One of the most important changes of a growing baby is his muscle development. You may think that babies are all fat and no muscle because they look so round and roly-poly. However, for the first few years of a baby's life, his muscles develop quickly, even faster than his bones.

Almost every new movement a baby masters means that more of his muscles have developed. From head to toe and from torso to fingertip, he gradually gains control of his body movements. This muscle control is called *motor ability*.

1. SITS ALONE

2. CRAWLS OR HITCHES   3. STANDS ALONE   4. WALKS

All babies start to develop their motor ability when they are very young. A baby wiggles and squirms, and after a few months he rolls over. He stretches his neck, pushes with his hands, and raises his chest. He seems to know that he is meant to stand upright as, time after time, he struggles to raise himself, falls down, and tries again.

By the time a baby is about six months old, he can sit up in a hunched-over position without support. Soon after he can sit by himself, he tries to move around. He uses anything that helps—he pushes with his hands, knees, and abdomen. Nearly all babies spend a few months creeping around on all fours before they are ready to walk on two legs.

The baby soon learns to pull himself up to a standing position. At first he may not know how to get down again, and he will be stranded upright until he's helped. Finally, one day between the ages of nine and 18 months, he pulls himself up, lets go, and takes his first step alone.

Once they can move around by themselves, most babies seem never to want to stop moving. Moving his body around is as important to a toddler as sucking was when he was new. He's discovered an exciting world of adventure and independence.

Learning to talk

One and a half years is an important age in the development of the child. Just when he has learned to control his body enough to walk around and explore on his own, he begins to be able to communicate with other human beings.

A baby experiments with his voice for many months before he's ready to talk. At the age of three or four months, he practices gurgles, chuckles, growls, and noises like "ga-ga-ga" or "na-na-na." Then, when he says "ma-ma-ma," his parents make a big fuss. He gradually learns that saying "ma-ma" brings his mother every time, but it does not bring his father.

He begins to understand some of the sounds his parents or brothers and sisters say to him—sounds like "no, no!" He tries to imitate them. His babbling takes on certain sounds that mean something.

Many babies communicate by pointing, or shaking their heads. Gesturing is easier than pronouncing words, and as long as they can get what they want that way, they'll keep it up. But eventually, they learn that words are more effective.

Words for familiar objects like cup, bottle, and blanket are the easiest to learn. Words for these and for simple actions like run, sleep, and go out are among the first the child uses. It

231

takes longer for a child to understand words like "soon" and "later," "far" and "near," or "yours" and "mine."

Sometimes a baby has a temper tantrum when he can't find the right words for what he means. A baby will sometimes use the "wrong" word for what he means. He may, for example, call all animals "dog," because that is the only word he knows for four-legged animals.

To a two-year-old, all ladies are "mommies," all men are "daddies," and all children are "babies." Only later is he able to divide people and objects into narrower categories.

Becoming a person

This is a hard time for a child because now that he can walk and talk, he seems more grown-up than he feels. He is more than three times as big as when he was born. He has learned many things about controlling his body. He can walk, take off

his shoes, feed himself, climb, and jump. He has learned to use a language. But emotionally he is still a baby.

He can't decide whether to turn to the outside world for pleasure and excitement, or to go back to clinging to mother. It's hard for the mother to encourage her child's growing independence and still be available when he needs her.

As he tests his new independence, he seems to be constantly risking serious injury. Most children fall downstairs at least once; most of them learn only after they burn themselves that the stove or radiator is hot. Here's where a new challenge begins for the mother. Just as her big job a couple of years ago was cuddling and protecting, her job now is to help her child become independent. If a child is allowed to experiment and see the results for himself, he will gradually develop confidence in his own abilities.

Between one and three, the child is beginning to learn how he fits into his family. He is learning whether his parents consider him "good or bad," whether they think he is strong and capable, or weak and helpless. And he is learning that there is a difference between being a boy and being a girl.

Around age three the child's family-centered world begins expanding to include the world outside his home. People outside the family—especially other children—begin to become more important to him. Slowly, and often painfully, he learns the lessons of getting along with others.

The foundations of his personality have been laid at home. Now he is ready to find a place for himself in the exciting new world outside his family.

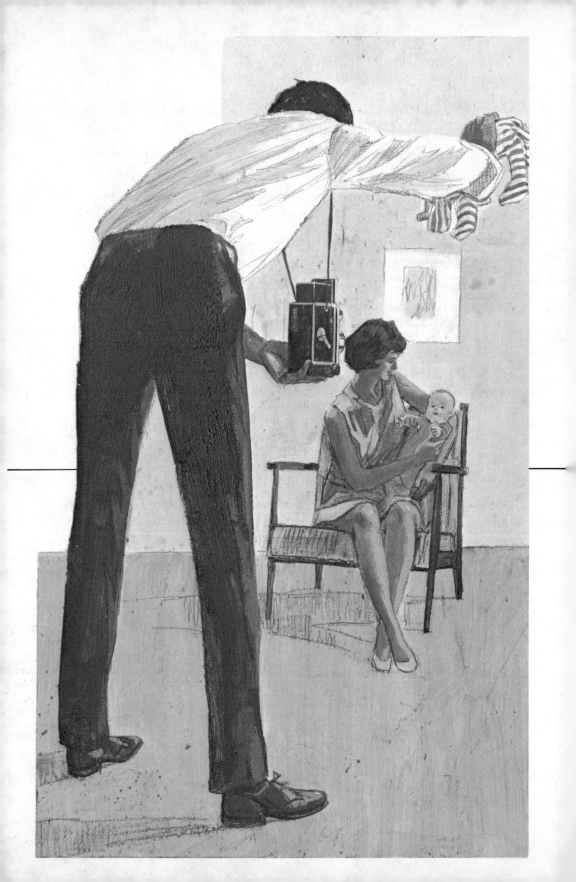

15

A BABY
MAKES
A FAMILY

No one can remember how his birth affected his family, but everybody can get some idea by watching what happens to other families with babies or very young children. Whether a child is the oldest or the only child, or one who came later, his birth was an important event. It caused many changes in the way his family lived.

This birth of a baby is often called a miracle of life. But this "miracle" is common in all the animal world. Almost as great a wonder is the family, which is understood only by man. A husband and wife are a family, but the arrival of a baby changes them into a "family circle." It takes a baby to

235

make a family that can grow from one generation to the next.

Each year almost four million babies are born in the United States. About 70 million babies arrive each year throughout the world. Despite these great numbers and the different customs and cultures around the world, all babies affect their families in much the same way. All human parents want a good life for their children. Most parents are willing to sacrifice to make a good life possible.

Why do married couples want children?

During the period of dating and courtship, most young people think about marriage but not necessarily about children. They tend to think of marriage as a union between husband and wife. When they become engaged and plan for their future, the couple has to consider that they may have children.

Most couples marry with the intention of having children, but not necessarily right away. Some may put off parenthood until they are better able to afford the expense of a family. Others start a family at the very beginning, and their marriage develops with their children.

The reasons why young couples want children are many and varied. Some married couples want a family simply because they like children. They know they love children, and they feel children make a marriage complete. They see having children as one of the important experiences in life, and feel that without that experience they have not lived a full life.

Similarly, sometimes a woman will want to have children because she feels that bearing and rearing children completes her feminine role in life. A man may also feel that becoming a father and rearing children fulfills his purpose in life.

Sometimes a couple is urged to have children by family and friends. A man with a strong sense of family pride may want a son to continue his family name. In years past, children—and particularly sons—were wanted to help on the farm or in the family business. This is still occasionally true today.

It often happens that a young married couple is not sure about having a family. They may have had little or no experience with babies or young children, and they have no reason to want or not want children. They may take the attitude, "If we have children, fine. If not, well, that's the way it is." But when a baby comes along, they are delighted.

The waiting time

Although a woman may have always thought she would some-day have children, when she is pregnant she may begin to have doubts about her desire to become a mother. She may have spent much time and effort in her education. Her job or career may have made her feel important. Now she may be-

237

gin to wonder about giving up those satisfactions because the rewards of motherhood are not clear to her yet.

The life process has been set in motion within her body, however, and a new human infant is being formed in her womb. As the days go by, she finds many ways in which her life and that of her husband are changing. They may not be able to go out as much. The wife needs more rest than before. She may experience morning sickness and a variety of other minor, but previously unfamiliar, complaints.

A man's feelings about his wife's pregnancy are new to him, too. He feels very protective. He is drawn closer to her as he seeks to shield her and the unborn child from harm. His pride in the marriage is increased. He looks forward to having a child.

The two of them are gradually moving toward a milestone in their lives. A husband can be of great help to his wife. Her need for love is deep, and he is the one who can best show her that she is loved and appreciated. He may need to comfort his wife, who may be unhappy about her appearance, diet, and restricted living. Pregnancy lessens the sexual desire of many women and this may lead to misunderstandings between the couple. However, if the husband is thoughtful and considerate, he can give a great deal of emotional support and physical help to his wife during her pregnancy. He should visit the doctor with her from time to time.

The months of waiting are exciting ones for both parents. As the baby grows inside the mother's body, its development can be sensed by the parents. Both the mother and the father can feel the movements of the growing baby. Even before birth, the baby is a member of the family.

The baby is born

When the baby is born, some changes in the home will already have occurred. A corner in his parent's bedroom or maybe his own room has been made ready for him. A layette of clothing and blankets is waiting. Relatives or hired help are often ready to help with the housework for a time, so the mother can rest and concentrate on the baby's care. It is all new and exciting.

Then the real changes begin to be felt. The husband and wife have just had each other, something like a town with a population of two. Suddenly that "town" increases its population by a third, and that one-third is entirely helpless, and dependent day and night on the other two of the "town."

The routines of living are changed, too. Someone may have to share a room with the baby, or give up his private room. Each addition to the family means less space and privacy for the others. The parents are not so free to spend money on themselves, live where they like, go out so often, or schedule their daily routine as they might prefer. Future plans and activities will be carried out with the baby in mind.

The changes are quite dramatic for the baby, too. He has suddenly emerged from a safe and secure world into an unknown one. But he quickly learns that there is someone there to care and fulfill his needs.

A baby knows only how to demand, because his world includes only himself and the vague figures who respond to his cries. Gradually things come into focus, and the strange new world begins to make sense. This is the start of a busy time for the baby, because he will learn more in the first year than he ever will again in any single year of his life.

This is a time of adjustment for the parents too, particularly with the first baby. They want only the best for their

child, but they get lots of different advice on what *is* best. Aunts and uncles, grandparents, friends, and books and magazines often give them conflicting advice.

It takes most couples some time to learn how to handle their first child. The baby demands. The parents and other children in the family give, share, adjust, and sacrifice.

After a few months, the strangeness wears off. The father and mother begin to find endless delight in watching their once helpless infant grow and learn to do new things.

Mother and child

The feeling of joy and excitement at the birth of her child sometimes leaves the mother temporarily after a few days. It is very common for a feeling of depression to set in. This feeling is popularly called the "baby blues." She may burst into tears for no reason, worry about the baby without cause, or fear that she will never regain her figure. She wonders if her husband is as interested in her as he used to be.

But her love for the child and her desire to care for him gradually overcome her fears. She learns to know her own child and his special needs. She learns when it is best to feed him, to bathe him, and to put him to bed. Babies need a routine, but mother has to include father and the rest of the family in the schedule she sets. Babies are sensitive to the feelings of people around them, especially those of the mother. Although mother and baby cannot hold a conversation for some time, they can and do communicate. Mother surrounds him with love, and he develops a sense of trust.

Father and child

A husband is usually proud of becoming a father, and continually amazed at the baby's development. Still, he may not like waking when the baby cries in the night, changing soiled diapers, or staying home because there is no babysitter. Some fathers adjust very quickly and learn to handle the baby as

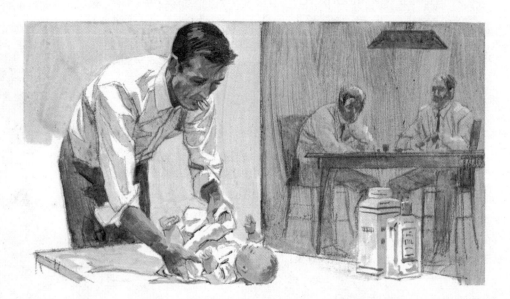

well as the mother. Others are not able to help with the day-to-day care, much as they love the baby. Some fathers feel clumsy or afraid they will hurt the child. Others do not believe it is a man's job to care for the baby.

As the father gets over the strangeness of a new baby, he learns what being a father means. He is every bit as important as the mother. A child learns first from him what men are like, and it is important for both boys and girls that the idea be clear and strong. The child depends on the father for three kinds of protection: against threats from the outside world; against fears within himself, and against too much protection by the mother.

The father provides a safe and secure home for the mother and child. The father helps control urges of the child which the child cannot control himself. He keeps a toddler from eating so many cookies that he gets sick, and an older child from attacking a younger one in anger. The father provides a balance in the family by protecting the child against the mother's natural tendency to baby him far beyond infancy.

Brothers and sisters

The struggle for the center of attention that goes on between children of the same family is called *sibling rivalry*. This competition between brothers and sisters upsets parents, but it serves a purpose. It prepares the child for the competition he will face in adult life. It is also natural. There is really no reason why the firstborn child should want to give up being the center of his world, or to share with another the attention of his parents. As more children arrive in the family, there are that many more competing for the parents' love and attention.

243

Jealousy is normal because each child would like to have all of his parents' love. Each child wants lots of individual care, and parents do not always have time for this if they are busy with "the baby."

When the baby arrives in a family with only one other child, there is a kind of special jealousy on the part of the first-born, particularly if he is under three years of age. The first child is used to having his mother all to himself most of the day, and his needs are usually quickly satisfied. Now, however, the baby takes much of mother's time, and there just isn't as much time left for him. If the mother can find even short periods of the day to spend alone with the older child, much of the friction can be overcome.

Children who are three to five years old when the second baby arrives also have to give up the spotlight. In addition, because they are old enough to do some things for themselves, the mother may depend on them more than usual. They may be put on their own a little more than they like.

Children who have reached school age when the new baby comes are much more able to enjoy the baby without feeling that they are being neglected by mother and father. They feel more assured of their parents' continued love. They are also busy with school and friends, and they do not mind so much that their parents spend a lot of time with the baby. Children of school age can be, and are, a big help in the family because they want to show they are "grown-up." They want to show their parents that they can stand on their own.

Older brothers and sisters who are well along in grade school or high school are usually delighted with the new baby, particularly if they have been given the news as soon as the parents found out a baby was on the way. Older children are on the way to maturity and are beginning to make plans for their adult life. Children of this age do not feel they must compete for parental approval, because they have had it for years. Besides, they are already striking out for independence. They are learning to share love and assume responsibilities, and the new baby is usually a natural object of their affection.

Grandparents

In most families, three generations are living at the same time, sometimes in the same house. Grandparents often have a special relationship with the new baby in the family. They usually feel that they can enjoy knowing their grandchildren without being totally responsible for their upbringing.   245

In many parts of the world, grandmothers are thought to be the family experts on child rearing, and mothers turn to the grandmother for advice. In the United States, however, customs in child rearing seem to change frequently, and parents and grandparents may have very different ideas about how to rear a child. Some parents may fear they will lose authority if they permit the grandparents to take too much care of the child. In other families, the grandparents may almost take over child rearing, perhaps because both parents work or because the parents are not living together.

Children and grandparents are good for each other. Grandparents need to feel useful and loved. Giving to and receiving love from a grandchild helps to satisfy the need for affection. The child, on the other hand, gains a sense of the life cycle of the family when he is in frequent contact with three generations. Oddly enough, some young people feel less of a "generation gap" with their grandparents than with their parents. Young people are often surprised to find that their grandparents have "young" ideas.

The growth of the family

The moment a baby is born, every adult in the family becomes one generation older. Husband and wife become parents; their parents become grandparents; and their parents become great grandparents. A baby brings a sense of time and eternity to the family as nothing else can.

As each child arrives in the world, he is the beginning of his own future family as well as the newest member of his present family. Families are born, grow, and pass on.

First there are two in a family, because the marriage of two people is the starting point. Then there are three when the child is born. Later there may be more. The child grows to adulthood, marries, and continues the family's link to the future by establishing a new family of his own. At the same time, the old family is gradually being left behind and, at some point, it lives only in memory.

Every family unit in the chain is linked by the children who are born into it. Children are the life and the treasure of a family. It has always been so. Two thousand years ago, the Roman matron Cornelia devoted herself to her children after her husband's death, rearing them so well they later became leaders of their country. While they were still young, Cornelia was asked by a wealthy lady to show her jewels. Cornelia called her children forth and said, "These are my jewels."